In the Shadow of Freud's Couch

In the Shadow of Freud's Couch: Portraits of Psychoanalysts in Their Offices uses text and images to form a complex portrait of psychoanalysis today. It is the culmination of the author's 15-year project of photographing psychoanalysts in their offices across 27 cities and ten countries.

Part memoir, part history, part case study, and part self-analysis, these pages showcase a diversity of analysts: male and female and old-school and contemporary. Starting with Freud's iconic office, the book explores how the growing diversity in both analysts and patient groups, and changes in schools of thought have been reflected in these intimate spaces, and how the choices analysts make in their office arrangements can have real effects on treatment. Along with the presentation of images, Mark Gerald explores the powerful relational foundations of theory and clinical technique, the mutually vulnerable patient–analyst connection, and the history of the psychoanalytic office.

This book will be of great interest to psychoanalysts and psychoanalytic psychotherapists, as well as psychotherapists, counsellors, and social workers interested in understanding and innovating the spaces used for mental health treatment. It will also appeal to interior designers, office architects, photographers, and anyone who ever considered entering a psychoanalyst's office.

Mark Gerald is a practicing psychoanalyst and trained photographer based in the USA who has written, presented, and taught widely about the visual dimension of psychoanalysis. He is a faculty member of the New York University Postdoctoral Program in Psychotherapy and Psychoanalysis, the Stephen Mitchell Center for Relational Studies, the National Institute for the Psychotherapies, and the Institute for Contemporary Psychotherapy.

"In this unique and remarkable book, Mark Gerald has given us a precious gift. Combining his extraordinary skills as photographer and psychoanalyst, he has produced not only a volume of rare beauty, but the most creative work to appear in our field in many years. This is a book to be treasured by therapists and artists alike."

— **Ted Jacobs**, MD, psychoanalyst

"With a keen photographer's eye, attunement to space, and a deep understanding of psychoanalytic theory and poetic storytelling, this book studies the complex meaning of the therapy office as a place, an idea, and a challenge. This book will offer insight to therapy professionals as well as design professionals interested in the relationship of space and feelings."

— **Esther Sperber**, AIA, architect

"These are compelling, impactful portraits of an international group of psychoanalysts that show the office environment as an important element of the therapeutic experience. Anyone interested in photography and therapy will be drawn to this collection of masterly images and essays by a well-known psychoanalyst."

— **Harvey Stein**, photographer, educator, curator

In the Shadow of Freud's Couch

Portraits of Psychoanalysts in Their Offices

Mark Gerald

Routledge
Taylor & Francis Group

LONDON AND NEW YORK

First published 2020
by Routledge
2 Park Square, Milton Park, Abingdon, Oxon OX14 4RN

and by Routledge
52 Vanderbilt Avenue, New York, NY 10017

Routledge is an imprint of the Taylor & Francis Group, an informa business

© 2020 Mark Gerald

British Library Cataloguing-in-Publication Data
A catalogue record for this book is available from the British Library

Library of Congress Cataloging-in-Publication Data
Names: Gerald, Mark, author.
Title: In the shadow of Freud's couch : portraits of psychoanalysts in their offices / Mark Gerald.
Description: Abingdon, Oxon ; New York, NY : Routledge, 2020. | Includes bibliographical references and index.
Identifiers: LCCN 2019015405 (print) | LCCN 2019016888 (ebook) | ISBN 9780429262470 (Master) | ISBN 9780429553073 (Adobe) | ISBN 9780429562013 (Mobipocket) | ISBN 9780429557545 (ePub3) | ISBN 9780367205980 (hardback : alk. paper) | ISBN 9780367206000 (pbk. : alk. paper)
Subjects: LCSH: Psychoanalysts. | Psychoanalysts—Portraits. | Psychotherapists' offices.
Classification: LCC BF109.A1 (ebook) | LCC BF109.A1 G45 2020 (print) | DDC 150.19/50222—dc23
LC record available at https://lccn.loc.gov/2019015405

ISBN: 978-0-367-20598-0 (hbk)
ISBN: 978-0-367-20600-0 (pbk)
ISBN: 978-0-429-26247-0 (ebk)

Typeset in Univers
by Apex CoVantage, LLC

Laini

Contents

■ Contents

Figures

■ Figures

Preface

Open the door into the private world of psychoanalysis. Inside you will find the rooms in which women and men practice their profession and the spaces that become home to practitioner and patient alike. Psychoanalytic offices are spaces that generally have remained hidden from all but those who come for psychotherapeutic help. The necessity for privacy in therapy piques outsiders' curiosity and gives rise to caricatures such as those found in *New Yorker* cartoons and Woody Allen movies, while the psychoanalysts who inhabit these spaces are often depicted as one-dimensional versions of the original Viennese Herr Doktor. Needless to say, these misinterpretations bear little resemblance to the truth of the talking cure. As a practicing psychoanalyst and trained photographer, I have been privileged to gain wide entry into these therapeutic spaces, and this book is a record of that journey. These intimate enclaves in which psychoanalysis is practiced contain the suffering of patients and the struggles they are working through with their professionally trained partners.

In the Shadow of Freud's Couch: Portraits of Psychoanalysts in Their Offices uses text and images to create a complex portrait of psychoanalysis today. Part memoir, part history, part case study, and part self-analysis, these pages showcase a diversity of analysts: male and female and old-school and contemporary. Fewer therapists nowadays fit into the Eurocentric, male privileged, heterosexual norm of yesteryear. Today's more colorful tapestry of healers is represented here, both in words and photo portraits. Along with its presentation of images, this volume explores the powerful relational foundations of theory and clinical technique, the mutually vulnerable patient–analyst connection, and the history of the psychoanalytic office. The 55 portraits of psychoanalysts in their offices were shot in the United States, Canada, Mexico, South America, the United Kingdom, and continental Europe.

I myself have spent tens of thousands of hours in psychoanalytic offices, mostly in my capacity as a psychoanalyst working with patients for more than 30 years. I have also been a patient myself in offices in New York City, California, and the Berkshires in Massachusetts. I have supervised psychoanalytic trainees in my offices and taught clinical seminars in these rooms. Since 2003, I have spent hundreds of hours visiting the offices of analysts in various parts of the world, where I have photographed and spoke with them about the places in which they practice.

When I first entered a psychotherapist's office and told that person about my problems, I had a new experience that combined feelings of confessional relief, newly conscious shame, and intimations of unreality. The office in which this experience took place, not especially distinguished as a space, became indelibly associated with the prospect of a particular kind of intimacy that has been rivaled only by the strange, wonderous state of being in love. *In the Shadow of Freud's Couch: Portraits of Psychoanalysts in Their Offices* is also the expression of that experience. Thus, this book is a tribute to the psychoanalytic office based on my own life and experience as well as those of others who have kindly shared stories and allowed me to view and photograph their therapeutic spaces.

Although the activity of a therapy session relies on the language of words, the strange, wonderous state encountered in the office is nonverbal. An analytic experience must undergo an imaginative transformation, conveying something of the essence of the emotional intimacy that has been experienced. Freud's great contribution was in shining light upon the unconscious. This vast realm of human activity that cannot be seen became the centerpiece of his theories and the clinical practice of psychoanalysis. So much of what matters in life is hidden from view. Dreams, slips of the tongue, free association, and the universal tendency to transfer emotions (especially those born of trauma) – from one experience to subsequent circumstances and to people not involved in the original experience – were all phenomena newly scrutinized and defined by Freud. His masterful efforts demonstrated the power and range of the unconscious and posited a therapeutic approach to some of the most resistant problems of mortal suffering. Yet Freud's genius did not make him immune to unconscious blind spots, in that he privileged hearing over seeing and thinking over feeling. This volume brings these neglected aspects of experience back into view.

I am the author of both the text and images in this volume and present the portraits of psychoanalysts in their offices for your perusal. Text and image here are intimate companions, which, taken together, may enlarge our perspective. This marriage of image and text mirrors the relational foundation of the book and psychoanalysis itself, in which both patient and analyst, interiority and external space, are in constant interaction with each other. I encourage you to see as you read and to read the book with your eyes open to the images.

Throughout the chapters that follow, I invite you to journey from the first psychoanalytic office to contemporary spaces in 27 cities located in ten countries. I have visited these places and photographed, in the first two decades of the twenty-first century, the psychoanalysts that appear in this book. Encountering an analytic office inevitably brings one into contact with the disturbance of human experience. Darkness pervades stories of betrayal, abuse, addiction, cruelty, and loss. The courage to enter analysis, to be a patient, requires a receptive partner to listen – and one who is willing to be affected by the relationship. The reward for the analyst is immeasurable in the flickering of the spirit to persist, to rail against injustice, to surrender in a cascade of sobbing, to carve out small spaces of dignity in the face of humiliating defeat. It is my hope that the time you spend in reading and looking will bring you a modicum of the deep rewards I have also received from writing this book and photographing psychoanalysts in their offices.

Acknowledgments

Spending the past 15 years or more thinking of, writing about, and photographing in psychoanalytic offices, I have been keenly aware of the importance of space in people's lives and the work that gets done in these places. I have written this book in many different rooms, and I am thankful for the opportunity that these shelters have provided for me and how they have become homes for the gestation of *In the Shadow of Freud's Couch: Portraits of Psychoanalysts in Their Offices*. I am particularly grateful for two buildings: the New York University Bobst Library and the Eldredge Public Library on Cape Cod. I have also found felicitous space for writing in many cafes and restaurants, especially Tarallucci and Land Thai.

I owe an enormous debt to the psychoanalysts who have allowed me graciously into their sacred spaces to be photographed and interviewed. There is a special bond that I have with these colleagues, who, in helping me create new relational images, are now members of a very special branch of my psychoanalytic family tree. Although I was limited in the number of photographs that could be reproduced in the book, I cherish all of the pictures and the memories of my visits to all offices. There were other analysts that sadly time prevented me from meeting with and photographing. That loss casts its shadow on this project.

Being a psychoanalyst is a great privilege, and I am reminded of this gift every day working with patients. I am thankful for the trust of all the people who have graced my office. You are my inspiration in your courage to wrestle with demons and to share your humanity with me. It is said that the child is sometimes parent to the adult, and surely the patient is often therapist to the analyst. You have helped me to continue in the struggle. I have also gained so much from candidates and analysts whom I have supervised. Their openness to learn on the path to become and grow as analysts is my standard for how to approach every psychoanalytic session. The psychoanalytic training institutes and centers that I have been affiliated with have provided me with communities of deeply caring and curious minds and passionate hearts that motivate my work and have provided me with many of my dearest friends. I found my professional home more than 30 years ago at the NYU Postdoctoral Program for Psychotherapy and Psychoanalysis, where I trained and am a proud member of the faculty. I also have been pleased to teach and supervise at the Stephen Mitchell Relational Study Center, the Institute for Contemporary Psychotherapy, the National Institute for Psychotherapy, and through the

■ Acknowledgments

International Association for Relational Psychoanalysis and Psychotherapy. I have learned from talented psychoanalytic thinkers and gifted clinicians in classes and supervision while in training and at conferences, consultations, and study opportunities with colleagues.

I have been very fortunate to have had my own psychoanalysis with three wonderful people; George, Sabe, and Paul have been my guides and companions through the sometime treacherous territory of my inner life. These men have been my psychoanalytic fathers. Thank you for giving me the room I needed.

This book could not have come into existence without the help of so many people. My photography mentor, Harvey Stein, has said that photography saved his life. I am grateful to him for bringing so much life into his remarkable and inspiring photography and for his keen eye and sharp mind in helping me to better see my own work as a photographer. My photographic assistants have made my project workable and have been a pleasure to collaborate with. I want to thank Shiri Bar-on, Jamie Saunders, and Ester Jove Soligue for being there with the equipment on the shoots and lending a photographer's eye to the editing process. I am so lucky to have found Gabe Greenberg, my printer. His technical art consistently finds the best possible version for each of the prints he creates. He is a master.

I have been rewarded to have psychoanalytic colleagues who have supported and nurtured my writing. Jody Davies gave me the first opportunity to publish in a psychoanalytic journal. My long-term former suite mate, Tony Bass, was an early influence in my desire to write. During his tenure as editor of the journal *Psychoanalytic Psychology*, Elliot Jurist encouraged and championed my work. I am indebted to Elliot for introducing me to Tema Watstein, who has been indefatigable in her pursuit of sources for permissions to quote passages. On a car ride between Rome and Naples, Sophia Richman and Spyros Orfanos suggested that I could write a book on the psychoanalytic office, text along with my photographs. They later introduced me to Kate Hawes, who became my editor at Routledge. Kate and her assistant, Charles Bath, have led me calmly through the complex process of bringing my idea into the fruition of a book. Lew Aron and Danielle Knafo, two prolific psychoanalytic writers, were very generous in their willingness to review my proposal and helped propel it into an offer to publish. I am additionally grateful to Danielle for introducing me to Maryellen Lobosco, who has edited the manuscript with great attention to bringing organization, clarity, and seemingly being able to know what I wanted to say even when I was struggling to find the words. She has made this book better.

Lunches and dinners with colleagues who are friends and talking on the phone with others are cherish segments of time that provided sustenance for my work and life. A special thanks to Barbra Locker, Seymour Moscovitz, and Craig Polite. I am grateful to many others who have shown interest and support for my work: Andre Acimen, Salman Akhtar, Jill Gentile, (the other) Marc Gerald, the late Michael Gerald, Barry Gruenberg, Lauren Levine, Nechama Liss-Levinson, Kim Roderiques, Zach Schisgal, Mark Singer, and Bonnie Zindel and the Psychoanalytic Society of the Postdoctoral Program for awarding me a Scholar's Grant.

My children, Jessica and Ben, their partners Adam and Sarah, and my grandsons, Leo and Joe, have given me the opportunity to be a father, a position that challenges and rewards in profound and complex ways. Life has been so rich because of you. My parents, Leo Gerald and Ann Dranow Gerald, would have been very proud.

Laini has been with me from the start . . . of the book, of the photography, of death, of life, of love. The excitement I feel in reading to her what I have written, in showing a photo I have taken, in talking about the progress or snag that I am encountering has never dimmed. From this boy to that girl . . . thank you.

PERMISSIONS ACKNOWLEDGEMENTS

Every effort has been made to contact the copyright holders for their permission to reprint selections of this book. The publishers would be grateful to hear from any copyright holder who is not here acknowledged, and we will undertake to rectify any errors or omissions in future editions of this book.

Chapter 1 features the poem "In Memory of Sigmund Freud" © 1940 and renewed 1968 by W.H. Auden, from *Collected Poems* by W.H. Auden. Reprinted by permission of Random House, an imprint and division of Penguin Random House, LLC. All rights reserved.

Chapter 3 features excerpts from *Morning in the Burned House* © 1995 by Margaret Atwood. Reprinted by permission of Houghton Mifflin Harcourt Publishing Company. All rights reserved.

Chapter 6 is uses material that was previously published in 2016 as "I wish that you could stay a little longer: Seeing the image in psychoanalysis," *Psychoanalytic Inquiry, 36*(8), 644–652. Reprinted by permission of Taylor and Francis, LLC.

Chapter 7 uses material that was previously published in 2016 as "The relational image: Creating a psychoanalytic photographic portrait," *Psychoanalytic Psychology, 33S (Supplement)*, S198–S214. Reprinted by permission of the American Psychological Association.

Chapter 8 uses material that was previously published in the *GDC Interiors Journal*, www.gdcinteriors.com/psychoanalytic-space-by-design. Reprinted by kind permission of the journal.

Chapter 11 uses material that was previously published in 2011 as "The psychoanalytic office: Past, present, and future," *Psychoanalytic Psychology, 28*(3), 435–445. Reprinted by permission of the American Psychological Association.

1   A tale of two offices and two fathers

I begin the writing of this book not in my office. It's August, and my office is on vacation. Nonetheless, although I temporarily stopped seeing patients for 50-minute sessions in my room on West 82nd Street, I had not fully vacated my position. The psychoanalytic office does not exist apart from the office of the psychoanalyst, and these two are somewhat analogous to the White House and the office of the presidency. A president is not always in the White House but never stops occupying the office while on the job, and even, to some degree, remains in office even after leaving the White House.

In classical Greece and Rome, early office holders literally carried their work with them. Being the holder of an office meant having authority and responsibilities and carrying out the traditions attached to a particular role. The movement from carrying an office to occupying a physical space in which an anointed one carried out an office's responsibilities first occurred in monasteries. Monks and nuns held religious offices and often worked in private cells to fully concentrate on their prayer and studies. During the Renaissance, the offices of artists and intellectuals were the studio, the study, and the atelier. Returning to the example of the office of the president, we have seen quite recently how an office holder may fall far short of their duties and responsibilities. Not all who have sat in the Oval Office at 1600 Pennsylvania Avenue have done it justice. Occupying space is not the same as occupying an office or being occupied by an office. To isolate oneself in an independent space for an enlightened purpose is at the heart of every psychoanalytic office, whether it is a private room of an individual practitioner or a private space in a university center or a hospital clinic. The professionals in these rooms are holders of the psychoanalytic office.

My early roots prefigured my occupation with the psychoanalytic office, beginning with an interest in my father's exemplary office in which he served as a Certified Public Accountant. He occupied a number of professional spaces during my childhood, but the office I most associate with him was on 161st Street in the Bronx, a few short blocks east of old Yankee Stadium, in a large commercial building. The heavy wooden door at the entrance to his office had a panel and transom of smoked glass. On the door, in gold-leaf stenciled letters, were the words Leo Gerald, C.P.A.

At some point in my adolescence, after reading Dashiell Hammett's *The Maltese Falcon*, I conflated my father's practice of public accountancy with Sam

Spade's private detective agency. That both had clients who relied on their expertise to solve their problems and worked in dark, mysterious corridors was enough to ignite my romantic teenage imagination. My vision encompassed not just the glamor but also the hard-boiled qualities Sam Spade personified. He (and my father to some degree) was not sentimental, had a keen eye for detail, and could be unflinching and coldly detached, even ruthless, in the determination to reach a perceived truth. In this crucial period of my adolescence, my father died, and the tension between the romantic and the realistic – the soft and the hard-boiled – brought on the anxiety that triggered my first visit to a psychoanalytic office. In the end, the glamor of the professional in his or her office never disappeared from my unconscious and is likely responsible for the turn my creativity took in fashioning photographic portraits of psychoanalysts.

I have been occupied by the psychoanalytic office for almost 50 years now, since I stepped into my first therapist's office in the magnificent Lewis Morris building on the Grand Concourse. The sensory associations with that visit are deeply held in the recesses of my unconscious. One of the most impressive of the splendid Art Deco buildings that lined the boulevard dubbed "the Champs-Elysées of the Bronx," the Lewis Morris in those days had a spacious lobby and a long listing of offices. Searching for Dr. Bloom's listing and office, I was filled with anxiety. I carried the dissociated experience of death that had been all too close, and at the same time, the anxious anticipation of relief from the dread of my own existence. It was 1969, and the war was raging in Vietnam; many of my friends were in the throes of addiction, and I myself was floundering. Dr. Bloom proved to be a solid, unflappable presence. He was a large man with a mustache and thinning hair, and he wore glasses. I don't remember much else about his appearance or his office accoutrements. Perhaps there was a couch I sat on. The room was smallish, giving me the impression of a secure space in which I could speak openly under Dr. Bloom's attentive gaze. I saw him for about six months and attribute to those weekly sessions my release from paralyzing dread. I also gained the strength to leave New York City and begin my dream of a California life.

These offices of my father and Dr. Bloom and the rooms of my childhood, both real and metaphorical, are the context of my own psychoanalytic practice and my office and how I both possess and am possessed by the psychoanalytic space. It is my contention that all psychoanalytic offices are created from the material of the unique spatial templates internalized in early life by each practitioner. Moreover, alongside this fundamental contribution to analytic space is the lasting influence of the progenitor of the psychoanalytic office, Sigmund Freud's rooms at Bergasse 19 in Vienna, Austria.

As a photographer, I have visited psychoanalytic offices in various regions of the United States and in Canada, Mexico, South America, the United Kingdom, and continental Europe, where I have invariably found unmistakable replications (sometimes quite subtle) of Sigmund Freud's iconic office. Despite cultural, theoretical, and personal idiosyncrasies, the shadow of Freud's couch remains.

HISTORIANS OF FREUD'S OFFICE

We are indebted to two marginalized figures for having memorialized that first office of the father of psychoanalysis – August Aichhorn and Edmund Engelman. Aichhorn possessed a prescient understanding of the importance of that iconic space at 19 Bergasse, and he was determined that it would not be lost to history and posterity. It was Aichhorn who recruited the young photographer Edmund Engelman to document the birthplace of psychoanalysis.

Aichhorn was a person of unique gifts and moral courage. An educator, clinician, and theorist in the area of juvenile delinquency, he trained in Vienna. Despite his relative obscurity, Anna Freud (1951) wrote in his obituary that "he was destined to become one of the significant figures of the psycho-analytic movement" (p. 51). Aichhorn had a calm self-confidence that remained unshaken by the impact of his young delinquents and criminals, and he was not deterred by the attacks of hostile government officials (A. Freud, 1951). His empathic identification drew him to work with adolescents whose behavior was antisocial and lawless, and his innovative schools for these young people used creative modifications of classical psychoanalytic techniques. Aichhorn felt comfortable with this marginalized segment of society – these children who did not fit the mold for "the analyzable patient."

Although Aichhorn was not Jewish and therefore was exempt from the dehumanizing Nuremberg laws, he was connected with the marginalized people these laws targeted. The Nuremberg laws stripped German Jews (and later the Roma and anyone considered "racially suspect") of their citizenship, severely limited their ability to practice medicine and law, required they register with the government based on arbitrary hereditary determination, and prohibited their intermarriage with so-called Aryans. Psychoanalysis was labeled a "Jewish science" because both Freud and many early psychoanalysts were Jewish. Aichhorn was especially close to Freud and his daughter Anna, but more important, he possessed an uncommon understanding of the historical significance of Freud's work. As Aichhorn's earlier pioneering work in delinquency indicated, he was a man ahead of his time.

Aichhorn, a member of the liberal Social Democratic Party in Vienna, met and befriended Edmund Engelman, a young photographer, through their mutual political affiliation. Engelman's part in preserving the history of the psychoanalytic office can be seen as equally propitious and fated. Engelman was the proprietor of a well-known photography studio and store in central Vienna. Although 50 years Freud's junior, Engelman grew up in the same neighborhood as the father of psychoanalysis, and the two men attended the same high school (Werner, 2002). Engelman, like Freud, came from a middle-class family of non-observant Jews. He was trained as an engineer, but as with Freud's training as a neurologist, his employment opportunities were restricted by anti-Semitism. As a result, Engelman became a photographer. In 1934, he documented the devastating impact of the Austrian government's crackdown on a workers' strike against fascism (Werner, 2002). The Vienna housing projects where the workers were barricaded were bombed and destroyed, resulting in the homeless women and children being captured by Engelman's camera. When the Nazis invaded Austria, Engelman destroyed the negatives for fear that, if found, they would incriminate him as an enemy of the Third Reich (Engelman, 1976).

Perhaps Engelman undertook the project of photographing Freud's office, which involved substantial personal risk, as the Nazis held Freud's quarters under close surveillance as a gesture of reparation for the lost 1934 photographs. Documenting the birthplace of "the Jewish science" was forbidden by the authorities, yet Engelman became the courageous recorder and preserver of psychoanalysis. In May 1938, 30-year-old Engelman entered the apartment building at 19 Bergasse with minimal equipment, using simple lamps and natural light to photograph the 82-year-old founder of psychoanalysis in his surroundings.

In the summer of 2001, I was in Vienna for a few days and visited Freud's office. This was my first visit to Austria, and I knew the city's association with Mozart, Beethoven, and of course, Sigmund Freud. But I also associated Vienna with the Anschluss of the Third Reich. Prior to leaving New York, I had spent some time speaking with my sister's friend, George, a Viennese Jew who had emigrated to the United States as an adolescent early in 1939. He had served in the United Sates military and was a very patriotic American. He shared his memory of Kristallnacht, the "Night of Broken Glass," a state-sanctioned pogrom that took place in Germany, Austria, and the Sudetenland. Jewish homes, schools, businesses, hospitals, and synagogues were destroyed, and many Jews were beaten, arrested, and murdered, while some 30,000 men were arrested and deported to concentration camps. George had never returned to the city of his youth, but Vienna remained a burning center of fear and rage in this otherwise mellow octogenarian.

His recollections were somewhere in the back of my mind as I strolled through the elegant Hotel Sacher lobby where I was staying and toward the concierge. I asked directions to the Freud Museum, and my inquiry was met with a puzzled expression on the face of this staff member, whose job it was to guide guests to places of interest or note in Vienna. I thought at first that he did not understand my question and thus attempted to repeat it in halting German. But the concierge's response, in clear and articulate English, confirmed that he did not know where the Freud Museum was located and hardly knew it existed. This remarkable and disturbing experience was heightened moments later when I stepped out of the hotel and immediately came upon the Monument Against War and Fascism.

In a plaza near the great opera house are four sculptures with antiwar and antifascist themes. I particularly noticed the figure of a bearded man with a toothbrush, hunched over in subjugation and humiliation. The sculpture memorialized a historical incident occurring in Austria, when Jews were forced to clean up anti-Nazi graffiti during the Hitler era. I found it ironic that this city, despite its repudiation of its infamous past, appeared to retain an indifference to the lessons of history, as evidenced in the concierge's ignorance.

This question of indifference accompanied me on my visit to Freud's office. What I found when I got to my destination were Engleman's images in the preserved architectural space. Most of the furnishings and objects were removed from the original office and are now in the Freud House in London. Engelman's photographs, which were not reproduced and made available until 1976, show the iconic psychoanalytic office in great detail. These images have loomed over all subsequent psychoanalyst offices worldwide, and indeed, they loomed in their imaginative form even before they became widely available. Engelman's experience during the three days of photographing Bergasse 19 is recorded as "A Memoir" in his book of the photographs (1976). Engelman and Aichhorn were in agreement about making an exact photographic record of every detail of Freud's office "so that . . . a museum can be created when the storm of the years is over" (Engelman, 1976, p. 134). What Engelman found at Bergasse 19 was a museum in itself, according to Fuss and Sanders (2004), two scholars who, along with others (e.g., Gerald, 2011; Werner, 2002), have teased out some important themes from Engelman's work. "Wherever one looked, there was a glimpse into the past," Engelman himself noted (1976, p. 138). Freud's collection of antiques were dominated by death-related objects, and the room was crypt-like, a place "of loss and absence, grief and memory, elegy and mourning" (Fuss & Sanders, 2004, p. 79).

Thus we must start with Freud to understand the psychoanalytic office, the first office holder, whose influence continues to permeate every psychoanalytic office even today. Freud died in London in 1939, a little more than a year after he left Vienna. His dying, at age 83, was protracted over a period of a few weeks. Freud had made a pact with his personal physician, Max Schur, when he treated him for mouth cancer in his early 70s: Schur promised his friend and patient that when the time came, he would help him to die. Schur kept his agreement with the aid of morphine, and Freud's death with dignity was a credit to analysis (Roiphe, 2016). But Freud's relationship and preoccupation with his own death began when he was still a relatively young man. Freud, the great rationalist, was susceptible to superstitious beliefs, what he termed "specifically Jewish mysticism" (Gay, 1988, p. 58). He predicted his own death on a number of occasions, imagining himself dying more than 30 years before the actual event.

The importance of his preoccupation with death, or what Freud termed his "death deliria," and its relationship to the psychoanalytic office are cogently developed by Diana Fuss's edited volume, *The Sense of an Interior: Four Writers and the Rooms that Shaped Them* (2004). In her chapter on Freud, written with architect Joel Sanders, she makes the case that much of classical psychoanalytic practice is based on Freud's avoidance of looking closely at death. The authors also argue that hearing is privileged over seeing in the design and architecture of the iconic psychoanalytic office. Using Engelman's photographs and architectural drawings of Bergasse 19 as a basis for their argument, Fuss and Sanders (2004) describe their own exploration of this space as "an attempt at recovery, at reconstituting from the fragments of history what has been buried and lost" (p. 73). This act of mourning comes from the same place as the "memorialization that so pervasively organized the space of Freud's office" (p. 73). Following the death of his father in 1896, when Freud was 40, he began to put together what became his collection of more than 2,000 antiquities, or exhumed objects: Etruscan funeral vases, bronze coffins, Roman death masks, and portraits of mummies.

Fuss and Sanders (2004) build a case for the presence of "survivor guilt" in Freud's office and quote from a letter Freud wrote in 1894 to Wilhelm Fliess, the person who may have been something like an analyst for Freud (Gay, 1988, p. 58). Freud indicates that although he has no scientific basis for his prediction, he "shall go on suffering from various complaints for another four to five to eight years, with good and bad periods, and then between 40 and 50 perish very abruptly from a rupture of the heart" (Freud in Gay, 1988). Freud lived another 45 years after this letter to Fliess, but his father Jacob died of coronary disease shortly after his prediction. Fuss and Sanders say, "Freud apparently felt that his father died in his place, prompting a labor of self-entombment that exhausted itself only with Freud's own painful and prolonged death almost a half a century later" (2004, p. 79).

The museum–mausoleum that was Freud's no longer exists as a working office. To pay homage to the master, people visit the original space in Vienna or the house at 20 Maresfield Gardens in London, England, where Freud lived for a year after leaving Vienna. The two spaces together convey something essential of the psychoanalytic office, its duality and the presence of loss. The theme of death and loss is prominent in the story of the psychoanalytic office, where the psychoanalytic discipline developed in both theory and clinical practice. Nowadays the psychoanalytic office has been decentralized from central Europe to England, South America, the United States, and various other parts of the world.

Although the space where analysis takes place has not received much attention in the psychoanalytic literature (Akhtar, 2009), professionals often experience strong emotions when setting up a first office, moving to a new one, or redecorating an existing space (Hershberg, 2016). Having a psychoanalytic office entails both providing a space for patients and having a room of one's own. The office both supplies therapeutic services and establishing a working "home" for the therapist. In setting up a psychoanalytic office, the practitioner looks toward both the past and the future. Looking ahead includes both psychic preparation and material resources. The plan or design of an office may be intentional or haphazard, but either way, the therapeutic space always is set up to meet significant unconscious needs of the analyst.

AN OFFICE OF MY OWN

My first private space was borrowed – the office of my supervisor, Milton Ehrlich. It was located at 5 Riverside Drive on the upper West Side of Manhattan. I had been assigned to this mentor at the outpatient clinic where I had been working part time in a fee-for-service arrangement: $7 per 45-minute session. Milt was a generous mentor. When he learned I wanted to rent an office after passing my licensing exam to work as a psychologist, he offered to allow me to see patients on the evenings he didn't use the office. I was just starting out, and Milt knew how expensive office space was and how little money I had, so he refused to take any payment from me. From Milt I learned about passing the torch of psychoanalysis on to the next generation.

Milt's office was a street-level room in a classic Art Deco apartment building off Riverside Drive. The room had bookcases filled with psychoanalytic texts, a couch, various paintings on the wall, and a large decorative fireplace in which a massive fish tank sat. I arrived an hour early for my first patient and inaugural session, pacing the room and trying to remember what Harry Stack Sullivan had written about the initial encounter in *The Psychiatric Interview* (1954/1970). All my mind could picture was the section in the chapter on "The Detailed Inquiry," titled "The Concept of Anxiety." There were no cell phones, no personal computers, and I didn't dare use Milt's office phone. There were no distractions. I was alone but also in the company of Milt. Picturing his calm presence and the smile in his eyes soothed me. The patient never arrived, but I nonetheless had been initiated as a practitioner in the realm of psychotherapy.

After seeing patients mostly in institutional settings for the first eight years of my life as a therapist, I finally obtained a private office. Moving into that interior space, I was accompanied by my first therapist, Dr. Bloom, along with the subsequent therapists and analysts whose offices I had frequented to share my fears and hopes, my dreams and terrors. I was also carrying with me the loss of my father and the closing of his office following his sudden death. It had been a humiliating blow to my family when a big accounting firm took over my father's practice after his death but paid my mother a mere pittance for his beloved clients. Finding a space for myself was an effort to resurrect his office and battle my shame at having lost my father and failing, in my mind, to protect his legacy. Writing this book is a continuation of that effort, just as every psychoanalytic office is partly an effort to restore that first office at 19 Bergasse.

THREE PORTRAITS

Associations with death have seemingly consecrated the psychoanalytic office, its practice, and the psychoanalysts who inhabit these spaces. I have been photographing psychoanalysts in their offices for more than 15 years, some who have since died, and there is no doubt that most of their workspaces reflect this preoccupation in one way or another. Luis Feder is a prime example. I shot his office in Mexico City in February 2005.

Luis Feder and an intimation of death

Getting to his home office turned out to be a fraught experience. I took a taxi from my hotel, where the concierge had warned me about the current crime wave in Mexico City. The driver took me to an upscale, suburban gated community outside the central city. The houses themselves looked like fortresses, and many were patrolled by armed guards just beyond the gates. After the cab driver dropped me off, I could not find any house numbers and began to wander around with an increased sense of anxiety. This led to a momentary association to the image of Engelman approaching Bergasse 19 under the suspicious eyes of the Gestapo, with a mixture of aspiration and fright, also similar to the conflicting feelings people experience when encountering a therapist for the first time as a prospective patient. Who was this man I was about to meet, and could I enter his office safely? When I finally found the residence, I was relieved to be buzzed in.

Luis Feder dressed with casual formality for the photoshoot. He was gracious and polite when he led me up to his office, telling me a humorous story about his father, a cavalry officer in Russia who had fled Minsk with his family and found a place in the Mexican military. Luis became less formal as we conversed, and he spoke eagerly about his interest in music. But while I was photographing him, something unexpected happened: I had a sudden glimpse of an old and infirm man fading before my camera's eye. This momentary perception of his disappearing image quickly passed. Luis wrote me after I got home, musing on the effect of the photoshoot:

> The impact of your visit on me was most stimulating and unusually gratifying . . . you have touched an unsuspected and uninvited basic ingredient in psychoanalytic practice: the question of space. In the case of the analyst, it is not only the visible space for both patient and analyst, but the peripheral space that gives me a particular "temporospatial" support, but it never came to consulting room considerations. . . . I have a special kind of musical register. Every person, memory or activity comes or is prefaced by an adequate tune in my mind.

I suppose he meant that his "musical register" was part of the metaphorical space afforded to him in life as well as in his work with his patients. Did it give him additional access to their thoughts or feelings? Or was it just a way of remembering them between visits? Some time passed after receiving his letter, and I realized I had not sent him a print of his portrait (something I do for every analyst I photograph). I tried and failed to contact Luis over the next year, and when I finally learned he had died, I recalled that "instant view" of his passing I was privileged to see during my brief visit.

At another point during the shoot, as I was inquiring about the various objects in his bookcase, he pointed to four large seashells toward the side of the frame in my camera's viewfinder. He told me he had written a symphonic choral using these shells and had named it "Shema: Themes for Survivors." The piece begins with the sound of conch shells and ends with the blowing of the Shofar, a trumpet-like instrument used in Jewish rites. After his death I thought of the Kaddish, the Jewish prayer of mourning and the association to those from the Holocaust who did not survive, and regretted being unable to share with Luis my last image *of him* before his death.

Luis Feder, Ph.D.
Corregidores
Mexico City, Mexico
February 2, 2005

Marilisa Mastropierro: an office like a hug

In June 2016, I photographed Marilisa Mastropierro, a photographer and psycho-analyst in training, in her office in Rome. When I arrived for the first photoshoot, I realized she had been there for just a brief period of time – her first office that wasn't shared with a colleague and her first in Rome. She was primarily attracted to the location, near the Tiber River, in a tidy neighborhood of elegant buildings, shops, and public squares. The new office had so much light and a rounded corner, which she described as feeling "like being in a hug, a parent's or loved one's hug, or the same feeling as being with an analyst." She was very anxious, awaiting the first session with a patient in this new space. She wrote:

> I felt that my patients would like it, that they would be fine. Obviously, until they came in, I would not know what they were feeling. Then the day arrived when I saw the patient who I had been following for four years in the previous office. That day in Rome there was a crazy thunderstorm. From my window I looked out expectantly for my patient. I felt so much anxiety, thinking he would get lost trying to find the new office. And when he arrived, would he recognize me in this new place? Would he feel welcome? I had so many questions and doubts. Each minute waiting seemed to have become an eternity. Then he arrived and I opened the door and accompanied him into to the room, and slowly we entered. He exclaimed, "Doc. But it's beautiful. I thought I would have found myself in a place I would not have liked, but here I feel. . . [comfortable]." His words allowed me to relax and be more serene.

Raul Naranjo: coming home

Raul was photographed in Madrid in June 2011, in an office that finally felt like home to him. He felt safe in the new office, as if he belonged to the place, and he experienced an emotional bond with the objects and the space around him. He said:

> When you are in the beginning of your practice, it's not easy to find a place in which you can feel comfortable, a place you can feel is yours. And this is very important in order to do good work. Your patients need to find a place warm and safe, and this is not easy if the therapist himself doesn't feel that way in the office. The beginning is usually (at least in my experience) traveling around places that are rented by the hour, shared with other people that sometimes you don't even know. This office was a place in which it was possible to create a home feeling. And I think it had an effect in how the patients could use that space and how they felt with me. For me, the most important factor in developing a home feeling was the location of the office, in the very institution where I was training as a candidate at that time. The bonds and the relationship with the institute and the senior analysts were crucial to feeling safe and supported, so it was easier for me to offer my patients that security and support. In some ways, the office represents something about the links and relationships of the therapists, their interests and passions.

Marilisa Mastropierro, MS
Piazza del Fante
Rome, Italy
June 8, 2016

Raul Naranjo, Ph.D.
Calle de Alberto Aguilera
Madrid, Spain
June 30, 2011

The creation of a new office or its loss makes a deep impression on the office holders of psychoanalysis, and they are intimately involved in this process. The inevitable movement in the careers of psychoanalysts, from the establishment of a first space to the interruptive traumas inherent in the course of a long career, is from vitality to loss. The promise and uncertainty at the start of a practice can settle into a middle period of relative stability and leads ultimately to the closing of the practice. But for every analyst who stays in their office for decades, many more move multiple times in their working life. Each relocation then becomes a juncture of the trauma of loss and the opportunity for a new beginning. This commencement honors the end of what no longer exists and can launch a new space that is never fully free from what preceded it.

PASSING THE TORCH

In my current office, I have none of my father's possessions. However, I do have three short, wooden bookcases that are replicas of the ones he built for my childhood bedroom more than 60 years ago. Moreover, I do feel that my father passed to me the torch of the office holder, and in that sense he has a place inside the space I occupy.

Mark Singer (2015) wrote a short memoir about a more direct and physical inheritance from his father – an actual patient. Mark and his father were both psychiatrists. One of his father's patients had been in treatment with the elder Dr. Singer for 47 years. This patient sought relief from an almost psychotic anxiety and came to trust Mark's father and felt calmed by him. He credited the senior Singer with having the magic to help:

> Just as my father was reluctant to leave his patient, the patient, as one might imagine, was reluctant to leave him. As it turns out, my father transferred the care of his patient to me, and he would now become my patient. Just before the termination of their relationship, after all the years, my father offered some final parting words of comfort to the patient he had known the longest, and with whom he had spent a lifetime. He said, with a knowing smile, "Don't worry, my son has the magic too." The words were comforting. To all three of us.
>
> (p. 102)

2 The shadow of loss and impermanence in the psychoanalytic office

The psychoanalytic office is necessarily accompanied by its own peculiar tensions and seeming contradictions. On the one hand, it is a place of sanctuary, away from the dictates and impositions of life, and a space that within its frame of the 50-minute hour approximates a timeless state of free association. On the other hand, the psychoanalytic office along with its office holder is continually aging and inevitably will cease to exist (Nass, 2015). This is the legacy of Freud's office, and its shadow continues to follow us. Part of the art of the analyst, reflected in their space, is to hold the press of these polarities in a dialectical embrace.

Analysts destabilize categories: inner and outer, good and bad, and darkness and light are replaced with the interpenetration and absorption by the unconscious of relational connections (Loewenberg, 2004). Within the enclosure of psychoanalysis,

- arriving at health requires attending to sickness;
- ignorance is the predecessor of knowledge;
- illumination begins in the dark; and
- acknowledging inevitable loss and the impermanence of life acts as a segue into mourning and creates the opportunity to experience a temporary state of deeper presence and connections with others.

Moreover, all these movements, reliably and without our consent, continually reverse one another. We are always in flux in the analytic office.

Clinical material from a long-term analysis is illustrative of these themes of loss and impermanence, and I will share one of my cases to demonstrate how. Moreover, I will exemplify these themes by looking at my own and others' experiences of the loss of a psychoanalytic office as a result of relocation, retirement, and death. In particular, I will emphasize the dimensions of darkness and light as they interpenetrate the psychoanalytic space of the mind, the relational matrix of analyst and patient, and the office environment and its natural association to the spectrum of loss.

CRACKING THE DARKNESS: OSCAR'S THERAPEUTIC JOURNEY

Oscar's analysis seemed to be going quite well into our third year of working together. He had first come to see me after a disturbing family therapy session that was supposed to be focused – or so he thought – on his daughter's persistent depression. He became very uncomfortable when attention was instead directed at his frequent disappearances from the family. He didn't like being scrutinized and felt "attacked" by his wife, daughter, and the therapist and their insinuations that he was up to no good. The truth, he told me in our first session, was that he would often leave the house in search of a prostitute, with whom he would use crack cocaine.

ESTABLISHING THERAPEUTIC RAPPORT

My first impression of Oscar, a tall African-American man in his mid-50s, was that he looked "so cool." I associated him with some of the black teammates on my high school basketball team and had an immediate feeling, despite being ten years his junior, that we could be friends. He commented on how comfortable the office felt and seemed entirely at ease in the early phase of our work, telling me about his life and struggles. He had a habit of pausing to remove his eyeglasses. He would then bring each lens to his mouth, moisten it with his breath, take a tissue from the box on the side table, and polish the lens. He would then hold his glasses up to the light for inspection and, finding them satisfactory, put them back on his face and resume what he had been saying. During these intervals, in which time slowed yet felt quite organic, I would survey what was in front of me. I took pride in my office as it was evolving, with furnishings, art on the walls, and objects I purchased on trips to other parts of the country and abroad. I also took the opportunity to quickly study Oscar and feel very pleased that this urbane, articulate man was part of my then fledging practice. He sat across from me and faced the one window in the room. I never gave much thought to the image I projected, backlit in the afternoons, during his sessions three times per week.

In his review of *A Beam of Intense Darkness*, a book celebrating the work of the psychoanalyst Wilfred Bion (Grotstein, 2008), Antonino Ferro (2008) riffs on the title, since darkness is the state that all three analysts – Bion, Grotstein, and Ferro – recognize as the place of origin. It is from this realm of shadows that "shreds of meaning" can emerge, if we can only tolerate the blackness. Ferro (2008, p. 867) writes:

> Like snails which produce slime, we are a species that continuously "slimes" meanings because we cannot bear the darkness of our not knowing. In the book's title we find a celebration of that "negative capability," the capacity, that is, to remain in the paranoid – schizoid position without feeling persecuted – the

mental state which, more than any other, should belong to the psychoanalyst (and, indeed, to any man or woman).

OSCAR HITS ROCK BOTTOM

While Ferro describes the positive side of darkness, the flip side of negative capability can manifest as a blind destructive urge demanding the lives of oneself and others – either literally or metaphorically. It didn't take long for Oscar's drinking and drug use to become the central topic of our work. I felt some confidence in treating these problems, having spent a number of years directing both inpatient and outpatient programs in substance abuse. Oscar's addictions were becoming increasingly punishing for him, especially the painful crashes of post-cocaine binging with intense anxiety, depression, and the agonizing craving for sleep. Finally, the repetitive cycle of using with prostitutes, feeling crippling despair in the subsequent days, vowing to never use again, and then finding himself again with a crack pipe and a woman in a seedy hotel room, landed him in the hospital. Years of alcoholism and drug use had taken its toll, and Oscar had begun to surrender. When he returned from the hospital, he embraced sobriety, started regularly attending Twelve Step meetings, and seemed on a new and healthy path. I quietly congratulated myself and him on our successful collaboration in defeating the darkness in his life. However, two episodes that occurred a few years later brought "beams of intense darkness" back into the room and into our work.

LOOKING DOWN THE BARREL OF RACISM

Oscar remained sober after his discharge from the hospital, and working with him during this period felt very rewarding. I learned more from him about what it felt like to be a Black man in a racist society. My office was located on the eighth floor of a building that housed a hotel, private residences, and therapists' practices. Oscar described his frequent experience of entering the elevator and watching White women move toward the opposite corner from where he was standing. The more he tried to show he wasn't a threat, by smiling or offering a pleasantry about the weather, for example, the greater the distress he sensed the women were feeling. He remembered that as a child, the other "colored" kids on his block would sing: "If you're white, you're all right. If you're brown, you can stick around. If you're black, get back!" He had been relieved as a kid that he wasn't as dark skinned as his sister and, therefore, could stick around. But all too common experiences, like the ones in the elevator, made him believe he didn't belong.

The first crack that brought the light in (Gerald, 2016) occurred on a day when the sun outside the window literally sent an intense beam of illumination into the room. This event occurred during a time when Oscar was talking more in therapy about his experience as a Black man. He had removed his glasses and was polishing the lenses, and in a moment, I saw him as if for the first time. He was Black! Somehow, all through our work, I had not seen that – had not deeply felt in the present moment that the person sitting across from me, telling me his life story and what it was like to be him, was Black. And in that moment, I also knew, more profoundly and beyond the cognitive knowledge I possessed, that I was White. People saw me as White in my office, and my whiteness was probably emphasized by the backlighting in that space. Moreover, race was paramount in this therapy office, as it was in all parts of Oscar's life and my life. I did not have immediate words to describe this realization, but it occupied my consciousness throughout the next few weeks.

BUILDING A BRIDGE ACROSS THE RACE DIVIDE

I began to feel that, as much as we had accomplished in therapy and as much as we seemed to be compatible partners in this endeavor, I was handicapped by our racial differences in taking the work further. Although my earliest associations to the Black classmates I had in elementary school were positive, and the middle-class Black families I knew were similar to my own, I began to recall disturbing racial incidents from high school. On my very first day as a freshman, as I was looking for my classroom, I was pushed down the hallway stairs by a burly Black kid. This was a rude introduction to the racial divide I later realized was rooted in economics. This kid came from "the projects," public housing made affordable for poor families, and most of the kids from the projects were Black. I then remembered how it pained me when I realized that many of my Black teammates on the basketball team were much more talented than I.

In this period with Oscar, I had a dream about him – the first dream I ever had about a patient. It was nighttime in this dream, and I was hovering in the air outside a building in his neighborhood, looking into the apartment windows, when I realized with a start that I had glanced at Oscar and his family. I awoke upset because my patient had entered my dream world. Here I was on the outside of Black life looking in. At the time I still ascribed to the doctrine of assiduously maintaining a separation between my professional self as an analyst and my private self (McLaughlin, 1995). Psychoanalytic approaches were in a state of flux, and the institute I was affiliated with, the New York University Postdoctoral Program in Psychotherapy and Psychoanalysis, in fact led the way in implementing new ideas. That program instituted the Relational Track of psychoanalysis pioneered by Stephen Mitchell and others. But at that moment, dreaming about a patient and finding a clinical use for it (Blechner, 2001) was beyond my capabilities.

I felt I was failing Oscar and thought he might need a Black therapist to go further in the work. I knew a few African-American analysts, and I told Oscar my thoughts about referring him. He replied that he had also been thinking along the same lines, but he wanted time to mull things over. A few sessions later, he told me he had decided to stay. He felt it would be too disruptive starting over with a new person; I knew him, and my willingness to refer him and to acknowledge the gap between us provided him with some comfort and reassurance.

A THERAPEUTIC BREAKTHROUGH

Shortly after this session, a second beam of intense light cracked the darkness in our room. Following another family therapy session, Oscar shared with me something he'd "never told anyone before." Once while he was a young father, his wife left him to take care of their baby daughter. He was high on drugs that day, and the baby began to cry. Oscar tried to soothe her, but nothing he did worked. The wailing became louder, and with a drug-addled mind, he took a pillow and put it over his child's face. The crying got muffled and then, as though awaking from a bad dream, he sensed the baby struggling for breath. He immediately threw off the pillow and picked up the baby, who coughed her way back to normal breathing.

Oscar was shocked into cold sobriety and also relieved that his little girl was alive. I sat in the room across from him, having difficulty fathoming what I had just heard. I had no words with which to respond. My breathing became shallow. Sweat dripped from under my arms. I fought to keep the images that were coming into my mind away from thoughts of my own children. Who was this man who had tried to murder his child? I somehow felt implicated in this crime. I was suddenly awakened from my trance by the sound of Oscar crying. "How could I have done this? I was only a teenager myself. I wasn't prepared to be a father," he said. "I have carried this horror with me for almost 40 years and blame myself for all of the problems that my daughter has had." Something new was created in the office that day. Tears were in my eyes. We were both struggling for breath. I felt as though a new phase of the analysis had begun. I started working with a Black supervisor to help me in my work with Oscar.

We continued to work together for another ten years. The work of psychoanalysis is often undramatic. Sessions are filled with the life of the patient, his or her daily experiences, and how they find associations to less connected areas of the self. Both patient and analyst struggle toward mutual recognition and contend separately and together with the barriers encountered along the way. Time itself becomes a player in the analysis. The couch and analytic chair begin to sag under the accumulated weight of the bodies they hold. Dust gathers in corners that the vacuum cannot reach and on the spines of books, some of which never benefit from a fresh intention of their purchaser to finally read them. The objects of the office age; some break and must be repaired or replaced. And time takes its toll on the two members of the psychoanalytic venture. Gray hairs are detected, eyesight requires auxiliary magnification, facial lines appear, and new clothing purchases are a size larger. There is an unrelenting and imperceptible force that weathers. The children of patients and analysts who were in elementary school at the onset of the work are now applying to college.

A CONSCIOUS AND CONSCIENTIOUS ENDING

One day, as Oscar removed his glasses and shined his lenses, he announced that he thought it was time to stop therapy. He was grateful and believed he had accomplished a great deal – an assessment I was in agreement with. We set a date to coincide with the beginning of my annual August vacation, and when the summer arrived, we ended therapy. When I turned out the lights and closed the door to embark on my four-week break, I only partially registered that Oscar would not be in my schedule in the fall for his three 50-minute weekly sessions.

Twenty years later and in a different office, I find myself every now and then removing my glasses to polish the lenses. I have come to think that these breaks from the idle position of listening with "evenly hovering attention" (Freud, 1912, pp. 111–112) are meaningful actions reflecting my desire in the moment to see my patient more clearly, in response to some perceived mutual blindness in us. But the gesture for me will forever be associated with Oscar and what we attempted to see about ourselves and each other in that office during our time together. He has left, but his presence remains as a hovering potential. The room is filled with many such hovering potentials. Every office contains, along with the furnishings and objects, its own array of presences from the analyst's history.

MAKING FRIENDS WITH LOSS AND IMPERMANENCE

Darkness is the origin state, and loss and impermanence are inevitable companions in every analytic office. The original psychoanalytic office was created to de-emphasize seeing, especially for the analyst. Auden's poem, "In Memory of Sigmund Freud," (1939) includes the lines:

> but he would have us remember most of all to be enthusiastic over the night, not only for the sense of wonder it alone has to offer, but also because it needs our love.

Darkness needs our love, our attention. T. S. Eliot (1944,) wrote that the dark is a place in which all must find themselves at last.

THE PAIN OF "MOVING HOUSE"

No psychoanalytic office lasts forever. Freud closed his own at 19 Bergasse in 1938. He resurfaced in London and even saw patients there before he died in 1939. At the end of each workday, in every psychoanalytic office, the lights are turned off. But the night with its darkness is the ripe time for dreams and the continuing work of analysis. The night needs our love.

As I was dining with a colleague one evening, she informed me that the building in which she had her office was not renewing leases but only accepting rent month to month. She and the other therapists who lease offices at these premises are fearful that the building will soon be sold and they will lose their spaces to practice. My colleague has been in her office for 16 years, and it has become another home for her. She toggles her life between weekdays seeing patients in a large suite with a wraparound terrace and stunning views of downtown Manhattan, sometimes spending nights sleeping in the office, and her weekends at her home in the suburbs. The rhythm of her life will be severely disrupted if she has to move. Thinking of her dilemma, I recalled having to leave my first real office.

I saw Gwen, the chambermaid, in the hall of the Hotel Olcott one afternoon in November, and she asked, "Have you heard? They sold the building?" It took me a moment to realize she was referring to the Hotel Olcott, the building that housed my office and my practice of psychoanalysis for 17 years. It had been a space I took for granted. I felt it to be my other home, and it dawned on me that it was not the permanent structure in my life that I assumed it to be. No, it was up for grabs, just another piece of real estate. I would have to move.

My world felt shaken. Yet denial quickly kicked in, aided and abetted by my colleagues in the building. There were almost 100 therapists of numerous persuasions who rented offices in the building. In every available moment over the next few weeks, on the elevator, in the corridors and lobby, and out on the street, anxious discussions took place in hushed tones. Questions were asked. Who were the buyers? Were we safe? When did our leases expire? Did we even have a lease? Some suggested that it could be a good thing. The tired prewar hotel would be upgraded. At the time the building was the residence of entertainer Tiny Tim and the Oscar-winning actor Martin Balsam. Max, 103 years of age, also lived in the building and spent his days sitting in the lobby.

The walls and carpeting and furniture in all these offices had cradled the countless analytic hours – hours filled with dreams of hotel lobbies, transference–countertransference impasses, and many other things. It seemed unreal and disturbing to imagine the Olcott as anything but what it had been. I had lived through two earthquakes in California and was reminded of the shock of being confronted with the fact that we did not in fact live on solid ground. Now, upon discovering that our lease had expired and we were on a month-to-month tenancy, I knew that I had to take matters into my own hands before being evicted. I had a recurring nightmarish image of hordes of analysts, like rats, exiting the Olcott building in mass hysteria and elbowing one another and tripping over their neighbors in a mad rush to the realty office.

COPING WITH THE UNEXPECTED

I found the perfect new office in a three-story brownstone on the Upper West Side, just steps away from Riverside Drive. The block was fully residential and quiet. My new office was a large square room with high ceilings, located on the parlor floor. There were bay windows at tree level and a fireplace. After months of furious looking, I had landed what I hoped would be my work home for a long time to come. But a mere two years later I was again dispossessed when the man

I rented from, an analyst himself living on the top floor, killed himself in a drug-aided suicide. His death was a shock and forced me to scramble for a temporary place to practice until I could find a more stable work environment. As an office holder of psychoanalysis, I packed my belongings, feeling like a refugee looking for a new place to settle. I was fortunate my patients came with me.

When psychoanalytic offices come to an end, how do analysts sustain the current of therapy through disruption and relocation? In my view, this is no different from keeping analysis alive from session to session. For both patient and analyst, the relationship, in best-case scenarios, becomes internalized in what is awkwardly referred to as an object relationship. Greenberg and Mitchell (1983), in their groundbreaking book *Object Relations in Psychoanalytic Theory*, broadly define this term as providing a place to explore the "confounding observation" that people live simultaneously in the external and the internal world and that the correspondence is not always one to one. Object relations encompass the feelings a person has about a chosen object (a person or experience with a person) and the emotional energy they direct toward that object through the ego or sense of self.

THE PSYCHOANALYTIC OFFICE AND OBJECT RELATIONS

Our relationship to physical space can be powerfully influenced by the objects we have internalized – as much as or even more than how we are influenced by the actual physical space outside of us. When I was moving from the brownstone near Riverside Drive to a temporary office, I brought with me a multitude of object–office relationships. They included

- the blood stains on the wall of the staircase in the brownstone where my landlord shot himself to death;
- the diffused light of late autumn afternoons in my office in the Olcott building, where I worked with Oscar;
- the massive fish tank in the office of my supervisor Milt in the Art Deco building where I waited for my first private patient who never showed; and
- numerous other associations to spaces I had occupied and that continue to be occupants in my sensory conscious and unconscious mind.

THE LONG GOODBYE

Marty Nass was getting ready to close his psychoanalytic practice when I photographed him in 2014. He was retiring from psychoanalysis and leaving the office in which he had started practicing in 1966. He had been in the inaugural class of the New York University Postdoctoral Program, a university-based model that became the first to train psychologists as psychoanalysts. On the wall behind Marty's chair was a black-and-white illustration by the artist Harry Nelson. He had probably created this image in the early 1900s, when he worked as a commercial artist for the newspaper, *The New York World*. The work, called *The Bridge*, depicts the Brooklyn

Marty Nass, Ph.D.
West 9th Street
New York, New York
July 12, 2014

Bridge spanning the East River and heading toward the skyscrapers of Manhattan. It was a gift from Marty's wife on the occasion of his 50th birthday.

Born in Brooklyn and deployed to the Pacific during World War II, Marty spent most of the war in a Navy ship. Still a teenager, he alternated between feelings of boredom and terror. The ship had a library with the collected works of Sigmund Freud. When he wasn't feeling too scared, he began his education as a psycho-analyst by reading these books. *The Bridge* was a symbol of Marty's success, rising from his modest immigrant origins in Brooklyn to the East 9th Street office in Greenwich Village. Similar to Tony Manero, the disco dancer played by John Travolta in *Saturday Night Fever*, the bridge (in Tony Manero's case, the Verrazano Bridge) is a symbol of an escape to the shining city on the other side of the water.

Norman Clemens, a psychiatrist and training analyst in Cleveland, Ohio, describes his experience of closing a private, solo practice of psychotherapy and psychoanalysis (2011) and addresses the loss of "the timeless quality in a fully open-ended therapy that enables patients to associate freely and follow deeply into parts of their mental life . . . without pressure for closure" (p. 351). Feelings of grief, rage, and sadness emerged as he notified patients. One patient he had seen for over 35 years asked for the decorative tissue box in his office, which he gave as a parting gift. As I read his account, I wondered about the absorption capacity of those tissues dabbing at the volume of tears produced in a 35-year analysis. Describing his own disposal of office furnishings and attempts to fit some of it into his home, he says, "I am experiencing a mourning process for my patients. There is an aching sadness" (p. 353).

THE SEEDS OF ENDING

One of the analysts I photographed in New York, Avgi Saketopoulou, told me how it felt to move after being in her office for ten years. I photographed her in her old office:

> Leaving an office where one has practiced treatment is such a strange and poign-ant experience: it's not just the years of one's own life that have been inscribed in the walls, one's own growth, own sorrows, etc. It's also that the walls, the space hold the ways in which you've sat with patients' pain, and hopes, and family deaths, and personal losses, and great successes, and incredible happi-nesses. Each treatment involves two people, two subjects, two unconsciouses, two humanities: but during the course of our day one of the two persons, the patient, leaves and another one comes in. At the end of the day, we are alone. The confidentiality and privacy required of our work seal this. In that sense, the space in which we practice is our only other co-witness to all this – so at the end of the day living and working in an office means that the space is your compan-ion; it is your only other partner; and [it] help[s] you hold the emotional archive. Occupying a space, going into a new office, is like starting a relationship. And leaving it is like a kind of breakup.

Avgi Saketopoulou, Ph.D.
St. Mark's Place
New York, New York
December 13, 2003

The darkness is the unknown that patient and analyst bring into the room. Illumination is provided by mutual recognition: that is, by seeing one another. I once met a man for an initial consultation and had the immediate impression we were related. He looked to me like a distant cousin. I imagined him as a far-flung relative, the son or grandson of one of my father's cousins, although not a person I had ever met. I somehow felt uneasy. The analysis of this man, over many years, proved to be one of the most tumultuous ever of my career. It became clear over time in working with him that I was not only dealing with this man, his disturbing problems, and our relationship in the therapeutic endeavor, but I was also wrestling mightily with my own internalized object relations that he had evoked from the start by simply presenting as someone who appeared to be related to me. Each beginning contains the seeds of its ending. The therapeutic relationship was an intense one. He left in a way that felt to be premature. In the memo section of the last check he gave me, were the words, "For: Failed Therapy." I wondered if seeing us as related at the start was, in this case, too close. If what I saw blinded me to what else was less visible. No analysis is ever fully complete. Yet I have pondered, as my experience has evolved, if we started anew might I have been able to see the work through to a better outcome. But it was not to be. When I think about him, I am reminded of the inevitability of loss and impermanence in the psychoanalytic office.

3 You can take the boy out of the Bronx

The psychoanalytic office is somewhat unique in being part workspace, part home, and partly the physical manifestation of psychological space. As a physical entity it contains objects such as a couch, the analyst's chair, books, and pieces of art, often displayed on walls, shelves, or tabletops. As an ethereal chamber it is associated with the unconscious and with privacy, and it resembles a house of worship or sanctuary to wish and perhaps to pray in – for comfort, clarity, intimacy, happiness, or peace of mind. Certain Jungian analysts conceive of the office as *temenos*, a Greek word for sacred ground: a place of secure containment, an enclosure, a womb, a protected sphere where one can go deeply inward.

The psychoanalytic office is a dream space to which clients bring their innumerable unconscious stories and fragments of REM sleep. In this room, their dreams seep into everything, in a manner of speaking. In the dream space the couch becomes saturated with the remarkable free-associative material from nighttime reveries of patients. Some are obvious, and a patient may laugh and say, "You don't need Dr. Freud to tell you what this is about" in relating his dream images of phallic symbols and dark canals. Others are frightening: "I was being chased by a gang of girls who wanted to beat me up, and when I finally made it to the lobby of my building there was a ferocious lion growling." There are dreams that are magical: "I was flying over the shore line and could see everything below. It was a feeling of wonder." Then there are the dream pieces like driftwood, caught just as the rest of the dream moves out of reach: "Something about a spring roll." Joined with the context of the dreamer's associations, these fascinating and puzzling experiences can become important touchstones in the psychoanalytic narrative.

The psychoanalytic office is also a dream space for the analyst, and it can be the embodiment of the dream of becoming a psychoanalyst. Having one's own office is a rite of passage, like a psychoanalytic bar mitzvah. Or the experience may be like moving out of a childhood home and into a space of one's own, tangible evidence of entry into adulthood.

The childhood home also enters into the dream space of psychoanalysis. We are all drawn to the familiar and must start from some home: a tenement in a rundown, overcrowded neighborhood; a comfortable house in the suburbs; a cabin in the woods; a unit in a large housing complex; a farmhouse. And although most people leave their original home, each in their own particular way, the places of our childhood remain centers of location, as when a compass needle initially wavers but always points back to its true north. These childhood homes may have been sanctuaries protecting us from the harsh and capricious repercussions of nature. But they also may have served as prisons, enclosing us amid loneliness, terror, depression, and misery. I was told by a patient who was sexually abused as a child that his house was always cold, the paint was always peeling off the ceilings, and nothing that was broken was ever fixed.

GASTON BACHELARD'S HOUSE OF IMAGES

Something of our relationship to these first homes shapes our journey through life. Moreover, even if we return home, paradoxically, we can never truly go back there again (Seiden, 2009; Wolfe, 1940). Thus it is inevitable that every psychoanalytic office carries in it something of the psychoanalyst's earliest experience with space. This formative exposure to physical and emotional space as a baby and young child occurs in the first home (or homes) of a nascent analyst. I first became interested in the relationship of childhood homes and psychoanalytic offices when I read *The Poetics of Space* by Gaston Bachelard (1958/1994). I am grateful to Dr. Charles Dithrich for introducing me to this volume in 2004. Since then I have read the book four or five times. First published in 1958, the work is subtitled *The Classic Look at How We Experience Intimate Places*. When I began to read, it became immediately apparent why Charles thought of this book as related to my project of photographing psychoanalysts in their offices. According to Bachelard (1958/1994), space (as experienced in childhood) transforms consciousness into dreamlike states. He says, "Our soul is an abode and by remembering houses and rooms we learn to abide within ourselves" (p. xxxvii). What more intimate space can there be than the psychoanalytic office to struggle "to abide within ourselves"!

I bought a second copy of the book after the first one became overcrowded with yellow highlighting and scribbled notes along the margins, reminders of the pleasures of reading the words of Bachelard. *The Poetics of Space* is written in felicitous language that soars and soothes and clings to the mind like a good melody. The book plays wondrous sounds each time it is read, and the reader has an experience of hearing something familiar and new simultaneously. Bachelard (1958/1994) says,

> the house we were born in is physically inscribed in us. It is a group of organic habits. After (many) years, in spite of all the other anonymous stairways, we would recapture the reflexes of the "first stairway," we would not stumble on that rather high step. The house's entire being would open up, faithful to our own being. We would push the door that creaks with the same gesture, we would find our way in the dark to the distant attic.

(pp. 14–15)

A French philosopher influenced by psychoanalysis, the surrealist painters, and such poets as Baudelaire, Rilke, and Poe (Aran, 2017), Bachelard trained as a physicist and then became a philosopher of science. He served as professor at the University of Dijon and then became the inaugural chair in history and philosophy of the sciences at the Sorbonne in Paris in 1940. Bachelard challenged the conventional beliefs of his day, such as the notion that knowledge in science increases as part of an ordered process. His conception of "epistemological breaks," the experience in which an unconscious obstacle to understanding ruptures and changes the way we know, was further elaborated on by Thomas Kuhn (1962) as a paradigm shift and by Michel Foucault (1964/1988), who applied the concept of epistemological breaks to such disciplines as medicine, sociology, psychology, and psychiatry.

Bachelard's later work moved away from science to consider language and imagination, and his own creative epistemological breaks moved him into new realms, including space and dwelling. His last book, *The Poetics of Space*, influenced architecture theory and makes important contributions to an understanding and appreciation of the psychoanalytic office. In this volume, the house – with its rooms, stairs and doors, attic and cellar, furniture, cozy corners, and position in the larger manifest world – exists in poetic relationship to the inner space of its inhabitants. The metaphor of the interior house is more than a metaphor, however, and Bachelard says, "The house images move in both directions: they are in us as much as we are in them" (1958/1994, p. xxxvii). The external penetrates our being and becomes an instrument that seeks resonance (and dissonance) in our travels through space. Memory and imagination are conjointly at work in our enlivened space, mutually deepening one another. Dreaming plays an essential part in this process because by dreaming, "the various dwelling-places in our lives co-penetrate and retain the pleasures of former days" (Bachelard, 1958/1994, p. 5). I would add that this process can also connect with the horrors of former days. It is the house's main purpose to provide the dreamer with a sanctuary in which to dream. For many psychoanalysts, this is the foremost function of the psychoanalytic office, to dream oneself into existence. Thomas Ogden (2003) writes, "The differentiation of, and interplay between, conscious and unconscious life is created by – not simply reflected in – dreaming. In this important sense, dreaming makes us human" (p. 19).

For Bachelard, as for Ogden, dreaming and poetry are linked. Both are expressions of, and means to, the elusive realm of transcendence. This unconscious territory for Bachelard is visited early in life in the first house we occupy. The physical inscription of the house occurs prior to the construction of memories. This engraving is dreamlike and made of the early awakenings of our senses. We see and touch and hear and smell the inhabitants and the space that holds them with its material existence, and they become poetic images. These impressions form a primal home for each of us, which becomes a dream house that establishes our orientation in space. Speaking of the first house, Bachelard (1958/1994) writes, "The feel of the tiniest latch has remained in our hands" (p. 15). Our body houses a particular "diagram" from sensory–physical connection with the early environment of objects and space and the people inhabiting it. The original experience for

Bachelard is a poetic reverberation with the immediate environment that is reimagined in dreams and evoked by poetry. His insights apply to psychoanalysis, in that it is the poetic image that has the power to free us from imprisoning personal history. In a psychoanalytic relationship in which there is mutual vulnerability to see and to be seen, these images can be rediscovered. We become more than the sum of our histories in experiencing the power of creative discovery.

Poets have written about this house that resides in the special dream space that cannot be found in so-called reality. In the poem "Ghost House," Robert Frost (1913) writes:

> I dwell in a lonely house I know
>
> That vanished many a summer ago.

The house has vanished, but the image remains. Margaret Atwood's poem "Morning in the Burned House" (1995) evokes the internalized engraving of a house that also exists no more. It begins:

> In the burned house I am eating breakfast.
>
> You understand: there is no house, there is no breakfast,
>
> yet here I am.

Evoking these early images of home, even ghastly ones, leaves the poet in a state of solitary delight. I am taken by Bachelard's intricate weaving of early life, the space that contains it, and the physicality of both, for the purpose of plumbing the depths of the human soul. His phenomenological approach, privileging personal experience and the language of dreams and poetry, harmonizes with the art of psychoanalysis as embodied by many of the practitioners photographed for this volume.

ANNI BERGMAN'S REIMAGINING OF VIENNA

Some analysts are well aware of their recreations of childhood homes. Anni Bergman's office in the Chelsea section of Manhattan is reminiscent of her early life in Austria. I photographed her in 2003. Years before, as a psychoanalytic candidate, I had been a student in Anni's class. She would bring out a platter of sweets for students to nosh on just as class was about to start, a gesture of gracious European hospitality that transported us back to Vienna, an appropriate setting for studying Freudian development.

Anni Bergman, Ph.D.
West 20th Street
New York, New York
June 6, 2003

Anni's office always has been in her home, which is an old, wood-framed, four-story building in the Chelsea section of Manhattan. The 10th police precinct is a few doors down the block, and at the time of the photoshoot, the area had been gentrifying, adding multimillion-dollar condos, high-end gyms, yoga studios, and gourmet markets to the neighborhood. Her building is an anomaly in this area, a throwback to another era. As I entered the structure and climbed the rickety staircase, I had the enhanced sense of a bygone time. Being in Anni's office was like visiting a home in Central Europe during the Victorian period. On one wall of her office was a photograph of Freud as a boy, which she inherited from a friend. In the photo Freud is pictured in his first home in Freiberg, Moravia, where he lived until he was almost four. He said about the place (Freud, 1931), "Under deep sediments, (living) inside myself (is) the happy child from Freiberg . . . who has received from this air and this earth his first unforgettable impressions" (p. 259). When his family left Freiberg to move to Vienna, Freud left behind everything he knew and loved: aunts, uncles, nephews, and playmates, all gone. For the rest of his life, he was haunted by the sense of something irretrievably lost. Years later, he said, "I have never got over the longing for my home" (Gay, 1988, p. 9).

In Anni Bergman's office there was also a painting, an image of a country landscape, hung on the wall across from where she would sit when she worked with patients. She associated, as she talked of this painting, to loving the mountains and rivers and the hiking and swimming of her childhood. She told me that her mother had died when she was ten, and she still missed her greatly. Anni had collaborated with Margaret Mahler and Fred Pine on a landmark book on the psychoanalytic understanding of early development, titled *The Psychological Birth of the Human Infant* (2000). This text, based on observational studies of toddlers and mothers, examines the theory of separation and individuation, when young children toggle between symbiosis with the mother and the need to become their own person. The tension between these two powerful drives was concretized by Anni's dog Sashi. The dog was perfectly serene when I entered her office but got anxious and barked loudly as I was about to leave, perhaps worried that Anni would accompany me out. Anni confirmed that Sashi had separation anxiety. As for the office itself, it was no exercise in nostalgia but a living presence of her childhood in Vienna. We can never fully leave our first home.

REMEMBRANCES OF A BRONX CHILDHOOD

Sitting in my office writing on a seasonably cold January day in New York, I am searching for proof of my contention that each psychoanalytic office has in it something of the analyst's earliest experience with space. I wonder what in this office contains remnants of my boyhood home in the Bronx. I spent the first 14 years of my life in the Hillside Homes housing project, the brainchild of the utopian architect and urban planner Clarence Stein (Parsons, 1998). Hillside Homes was designed in the early 1930s in the Williamsbridge section of the North Bronx, a government-sponsored complex providing affordable housing for Italian, Irish, and

Jewish immigrants fleeing the crowded slums of the Lower East Side and other neighborhoods. Hillside Homes became their piece of America.

Stein's vision was to create communities, and Hillside Homes became such a community, covering five blocks with low-rise brick buildings, interconnected courtyards, a large playground with basketball and handball courts, numerous open spaces, common rooms for workshops, clubs, and a nursery school. One could walk through the buildings and courtyards from Wilson Avenue to Eastchester Road in this contained world without ever walking onto the main streets that surrounded our utopian enclave. Living in this community afforded space and physical experience to coincide with, and to be used by, the emerging developmental prompts of its children. The passageways between the courtyards were transitions between states of being. They were small tunnels and could serve as enclosures, a site for the growth of competitive energy in a spirited version of handball that was called Jack, Queen, King. The tunnels also represented secrets and, at times, the dangerous territory between childhood and adolescence. Rituals of sexual play; experiments in smoking, drinking, and drugs; and a hovering specter of violence loomed in those tubular channels.

Psychoanalytic offices are also sanctuary spaces but are not divorced from the world outside. Yet they must be kept safe to provide the oneiric climate needed for analysis to take place. Scanning my office and thinking about my childhood home, I was reminded of one of the first attempts I made to possess space. For most of my childhood, I shared a bedroom with my sister; my parents slept in the living room until we moved a few blocks down the hill to a two-bedroom apartment where my parents had their own room. When my sister became an adolescent and I was getting close to puberty, my father built a partition, providing each of us with our own personal space. I immediately began to cover the wall next to my bed with color pictures from the magazines of the day. I chose photographic portraits from the pages of *Life* and *Sports Illustrated*.

In my office now is an antique wooden bureau. With a slight tilt of my head, I can see the bureau. When a patient is on the couch, that tilt is the physical representation of an internal state of reverie. I am thinking, and my head moves upward to find the thoughts. On the marble top of the bureau rests a carved, walnut-framed mirror. I have postcards around the edges of the mirror tucked into the space where the glass inserts in the frame. There are currently 13 cards on display. They include some admired figures (as were the sports heroes exhibited on the wall in my childhood bedroom), along with portrait images that intrigue me: Greta Garbo in black, a profile silhouette of Alan Ginsburg at his writing desk, 16-year-old Lew Alcindor palming a basketball in Harlem, Franz Kafka with haunted eyes, Eleanor Roosevelt at the United Nations, a proper Frenchman weeping in June 1940 as the Germans enter Paris, and the joyous smiles of two North African girls alight in play. I feel in the company of friendly spirits. Together they create a space for me to be with my thoughts, feelings, and associations. I can dive deep and swim broadly in their presence as I am experiencing my patients' own deep explorations.

I am reminded of Jody Davies, who described how she felt held in her psycho-analytic chair with her books nearby. She told me they provided her with a tangible connection to the field. The placement of her bookcase behind her helped create a surrounding embrace with her psychoanalytic ancestors and community. "It's a way of not feeling so alone," she said (personal communication, July 23, 2003).

I have five bookcases in my office. Two of them, seven feet tall each, flank the bureau. Over time I needed more space for new titles. Initially I had brought in low bookcases, 24 inches high, which were added one by one. My paternal grandfather had been a carpenter, and Grandpa Joseph had passed his talent down to his two sons, my father and uncle. In his retirement years, gifted Uncle Toby built intricate dollhouses with detailed flourishes. My father's bent was more functional: shelving, a toy chest, boards for the tracks of my electric train set, and two low, open cabinets that held my first books. The shorter bookcases in my office are very like the ones my father built. I count 12 wooden pieces of furniture in pine, walnut, and cherry. The sight, touch, and smell of wood are keenly suggestive for me. There is the carpenter's tool of a wooden plane that belonged to my grandfather, and it serves as a book end on one of the low cabinets. I am in the realm of Bachelard's first house.

THE PAIN OF ENTRAPMENT, LOSTNESS, AND LOSS

Early places of residence and the poetic imagery called forth by living in these spaces enter the psychoanalytic office in the dreams of patients. A patient in his 40s talks about two recurring dreams from childhood. In the first dream, he is on a winding path that leads to his home. But no matter how far he travels, he cannot find the connecting road that will take him to his father. His parents divorced when he was young. In the dream he is terribly frustrated on this interminable journey whose end is always out of reach. In the second relentless dream, he is enclosed in a room where he can hear exciting life taking place outside. He tries to find an exit, but there is no door, and he realizes that the room has been nailed shut. He screams for someone to hear him and let him out so he can join in the festivities.

The patient sits on the couch as he recalls these dreams. He fiddles with the tassels on the throw pillows that surround him. Sometimes he picks at the buttons on the tufted seat of the couch. Although clearly a nervous habit, I track the frequency and intensity of these actions with the correspondence of expressions of frustration and sense of failure in his life. By many accounts, he is a very successful man and capable of experiencing pleasure and deep engagement. But he longs for a more sustained sense of growth and direction that is always elusive. He uses the term "passionate abandon" to express what he yearns for, but he's stuck in his nailed-up room and lost on his winding path to nowhere. I'm very fond of this man and closely identify with his creative needs. I imagine his fiddling and picking to be that of a safe cracker, desperately struggling to find the combination to release him so he can find his way home. Time is running out in this imagined scenario, but much more for me, 25 years his senior. I fretted early on in our work, feeling so connected to his need and pressure to break free. But over time, I have come to feel more at home with my patient, as we both move along on our road to find the creative space that resides deep in childhood homes.

I connect this patient's desire to get home with singer-songwriter Lucinda Williams's bittersweet lament, "Lake Charles," about the longing for one's place of origin. She has said the song was inspired by the death of a former boyfriend (Moser, 2017), who longed to go back to Lake Charles. But she herself was born in Lake Charles, Louisiana, and in this song she conveys the aching love and longing of someone who wants to return to a beloved place from whence she came. Williams spent a significant part of her childhood in New Orleans, raised mostly by her father, a poet and literature professor. His poem "The Shrinking Lonesome Sestina" (M. Williams, 2000, p. 38) begins, "Somewhere in everyone's head something points toward home." The song by Lucinda Williams contains specific locations and details that authorize her as a person from the American South and particularly from Lake Charles. The lyrics mention Nacogdoches in East Texas, Lafayette and Baton Rouge, the Louisiana Highway, and Lake Pontchartrain. For part of the trip the song takes the listener traveling in a yellow El Camino. Lucinda sings that there's music playing in the car, by the legendary blues artist Howlin' Wolf. Like his sandpaper growl, Lucinda Williams' voice is cracking and raspy but one that's "slowly drowning in honey" (Schilling, 2013). On some of her slower songs, Williams sounds like something between slightly drunk and crying. Her voice carries a poignant, story-telling quality familiar in the offices of therapists, who regularly listen to the sorrows of others.

This longing for home is the theme of a psychoanalytic paper by Henry Seiden (2009), also a boy from the Bronx, who uses a wide range of narratives (literary, cultural, historical, clinical, and personal) to demonstrate this topic "largely ignored in the psychoanalytic literature" (p. 191). According to Seiden,

> To be sure, the longing for home is a longing to repair two kinds of separations – one in place, one in time. A home lost to time is no longer there and cannot be. This is true of my childhood Bronx. It is gone – along with my parents, my childhood friends, the neighbors on my block, along with the smell of my grandmother's soup cooking on the stove in the kitchen of our fourth floor apartment.
>
> (p. 196)

This inaccessible home exists alongside Bachelard's felicitous home; the dance between these two – their intertwined movement – is present in every psychoanalysis and every psychoanalytic office. A few years ago as I was preparing a presentation (Gerald, 2013) that was the forerunner of this chapter, I returned to my childhood home of Hillside Homes. I had not visited the neighborhood in many years, and the night prior to the visit, I had this dream:

> I was in a big beautiful office, decorated with art, and I was showing my analyst around the space. He was very appreciative of the art, especially a photograph

of me and, nearby, cardboard cutouts of my father and mother. In fact, he was enthralled and started to dance a wild Hasidic folk dance. The dream space shifted to an apartment like my mother's or one we had previously lived in. There was lots of stuff around: unused, not cared for, breaking, old, dusty, in disrepair: objects from childhood, remembered fondly, possibly my son's childhood. Also in this room were broken lights, an old TV, and a *Star Wars* spaceship and space station that was falling apart. In another shift in the dream, I was sitting on the ground with old Native American men with blankets around our shoulders. We were drinking; we were people without a home.

MY FIREHOUSE DREAM

The next day at Hillside Homes I was especially interested in seeing and photographing the firehouse on Eastchester Road. As a child I could see this firehouse through the window of our living room in that first apartment I lived in. This view provided endless hours of engagement and fantasy as I watched the firemen and the trucks and especially the graceful and powerful turning of the magnificent red hook and ladder. As a boy, I wanted to be a firefighter, though I never entered that building that was so special for me. I was determined on this visit to finally get inside. Fortunately, a man came out of the building and invited me in for a tour, and I was transported back in time, more than half a century. This experience was what I had imagined and both more and less than what I had imagined. The trucks were awesome vehicles that exuded power and majesty, but up close they showed the scars of their many rescue missions. The uniforms, gadgets, and tools strewn on the floor and walls of the house were exotic and seemed to exist in a larger gauge than would befit most normal-size humans. The inner sanctum of the building, its common room (and the focus of much of my childhood fantasy), was now home to a half a dozen men lounging in bent postures on a worn couch near an industrial-size kitchen.

I felt a sad disappointment as a romantic and colorful image shattered into what seemed like a faded room of displaced people, including myself. The firemen were smaller in their stature, from my adult perspective, and despite their offering me a cup of coffee, my sense of their world weariness, combined with and concealing a tangible guarded hostility because their refuge had been infringed, compelled me to decline and leave the premises quickly. The dangers in the tunnels of Hillside Homes and the old homeless men in my dream were suddenly present in this place.

I think the dream is about growing old, falling into decay, and finally into death and dissolution, just as the objects of our past do, both in real life and in the metaphorical dream house. And was there in my early desire to be a fireman, the seeds of my career as a psychoanalyst, a rescuer of people in need? Over time, all psychoanalysts become battle scarred, like the once-pristine red fire trucks. The most idealistic among us cannot maintain the perfect dream that is the hallmark of childhood innocence.

SAUDADE

I bring all this company, originating in the Bachelardian imagination of my child-hood, into the life of my own psychoanalytic office. My current workspace in the third full-time office I have occupied in my 30 years of practice. It is a room of some consistency. I have had the couch, a few pieces of art, a couple of lamps, and some of the books since the first day. And although I have had each of the offices painted, and more than once, it has always been with Benjamin Moore #2125–50, a soothing gray called "Sweet Innocence." Over the years pieces of fur-niture have been replaced, and some furniture has been added, along with new art and objects. A fairly recent addition was a small, colorful paperweight I had found in an antique stall in Rio de Janeiro. On the day prior to obtaining this item, I had photographed a Brazilian analyst, Renato Barauna, who has a very similar item in his office and told me it had been his father's. They were both psychiatrists, and the paperweight held great meaning for him.

I had learned while in Brazil about the concept of *saudade*, a very important yet untranslatable word for Brazilians and other Portuguese speakers. *Saudade* is something like a bittersweet nostalgia for something that is missed. It expresses a longing for someone or something that may even be present but that cannot be possessed (Steven Knoblauch, personal communication, April 6, 2013). The pres-ence of absence is what gives *saudade* its deep and incongruous melancholic pleasure. It is what Bachelard conveys in his *Poetics of Space* and what Lucinda Williams sings about in "Lake Charles." Many examples of *saudade* can be found in Seiden's "Longing for Home" (2009). In my case, despite leaving the Bronx decades ago, the Bronx has never left me, and yet I too long for home. My dream, the words of the poets, the stories and dreams of my patients are all depositories of *saudade*. These places of our beginning are the core of us, yet we can never return to them. Even so, this core is the fuel of our life and seems to hold the key to whom we really are. But we can't return to that place, we can't find the key, and we can't go home again. And even in the dream space, home is an illusion. Ultimately we are missing something that is both real and does not really exist.

Renato Barauna, MD
Rua Fonte da Saudade
Rio de Janeiro, Brazil
February 1, 2013

4   Photography and psychoanalysis

Two types of memorial art

I have no photograph from the day when, as a young boy, I got lost on a family outing in Bear Mountain State Park. We were walking back to the parking lot when I stopped to watch a group of men playing soccer. I couldn't have been more than five or six and remember being intrigued, almost to the point of hypnotism, by the players' concerted effort of running after the ball, kicking it away, and running toward it again. I had no idea what the game was called or how it was played, but I found the rhythmic play of intense physical energy, focused on the white, round sphere, continuously in motion, to be captivating. It was a warm day, probably in the summer, and although I have no memory of anything that preceded the moment I stopped to watch the soccer game, I feel sure it had been an idyllic day with my parents in the country.

Only 40 miles north of the Bronx, Bear Mountain was a popular place for people to get away from the sweltering heat of small city apartments with no air conditioning. Since we didn't have a car, my family probably drove up to Bear Mountain that day with Uncle Aaron and Aunt Eva, whom we often accompanied on weekend day trips, riding in their Buick sedan. In the park were picnic areas, hiking trails, playing fields, and a giant carousel featuring beautifully hand-painted scenes of the forest and carvings of animals whose natural habitat was the Hudson River Valley.

My memory easily focuses like a camera lens on that moment of that day when I came out of a trance of watching the soccer players. I immediately became aware that I had lost time, and the loss felt immense because, along with the minutes and seconds that expired in my dreamlike state, I had lost my family. They apparently had continued to the parking lot without me. A feeling of fear and then panic descended on and enveloped me as I searched desperately for a familiar face, nowhere to be found. The next thing I recall is being in the front seat of a police car, but probably the car of a park ranger, and trying not to cry as he asked me for my name and where I lived. He got on the walkie-talkie with park headquarters, and when we arrived there, I was reunited with my parents. When they picked me up and embraced me, I felt relieved but mostly very happy and safe.

There is no photographic record of that day, although Uncle Aaron was an avid photographer and would likely have had his camera along with him. Thousands of family photos exist, in dozens of shoe boxes and albums, but none bear witness to the Bear Mountain excursion and its emotional range of feeling: pleasure, belonging, fascination, being lost in thought, terror, and relief, all occurring on one day in a man's boyhood. How much of my memory is accurate? What have I censored or enhanced to generate a more coherent, pleasing, or tolerable rendition of events? If one or more photographs were available, would the memory be modified or even cease to be such a lasting and meaningful one?

PHOTOGRAPHS AS RECORDS

From its onset in the early nineteenth century, photography became a way to accurately record aspects of reality. Through the mechanical and scientific means of the instrument of the camera and the chemicals used to process images, evidence of the world could be documented, beginning with the first daguerreotypes, moving through George Eastman's film roll ("You push the button, we do the rest"), and culminating in the contemporary and ubiquitous smartphone, where everyone is a photographer and everything is recorded.

According to John Szarkowski (1973), the earliest daguerreotype photographs were used for ". . . recording the faces of millions of people." He goes on to say, "Of the countless thousands of daguerrotypes [sic] that survive, not one in a hundred shows a building or a waterfall or a street scene" (p. 14). Moreover, in the early history of photography, taking a photograph of a deceased loved one was a normal part of American and European culture, even into the early twentieth century. These memorial or mourning portraits were created as a visual remembrance and served as an aid in grieving. They were living proof that the deceased person had (once) been here. A more recent example of memorializing the dead (and the lost) through photography was seen in the aftermath of the World Trade Center attacks of September 11, 2001. Families of missing people put up thousands of posters with photos and descriptions of their loved ones. Parks in New York City, such as the one in Union Square, became gathering points for people to come together, share stories, and lend support. On one display was a poster with a photograph of a family with their arms around one another. The caption on the top of the poster read, "Have You Seen Me?" And a line was drawn to the person who appeared to be the father of the family. Some additional information was provided including the missing person's name and a contact phone number. The final line said: "1 World Trade Center, 38th Floor."

While writing this chapter in the library, I was interrupted by my smartphone showing me a call was coming in. At the library I normally ignore a call, but I noticed my analyst's name on the screen, so I left the reading room and picked up the call. My analyst told me he wouldn't be able to keep our scheduled session later that day because he was in the hospital emergency room with "a concernedly low heart rate." He went on to say that he hadn't been worried when this problem first manifested; he thought that maybe it was Lyme disease, but he was now getting a little bit upset. He joked about the hospital personnel in a manner that was very familiar to me as a means of quelling rising anxiety. I told him to take care of himself, to trust the doctors, and not to worry about me. But I myself was worried about him. I was consoled by the fact that I had a photograph of him, an enlarged print in my series of portraits of psychoanalysts, and I found solace in the fact that I also had given him a copy.

In a recent article, novelist and essayist Geoff Dyer (2017) references literary theorist and philosopher Roland Barthes to muse on "The Mysteries of Our Family Snapshots." He says: "a single pic(ture) of his [Barthes's] recently deceased mother, the so-called 'Winter Garden Photograph,'" captured what he considered her defining characteristic – in Barthes's words, "the assertion of a gentleness." For Dyer this realization, achieved through a special kind of looking, is "the essence of photography." Dyer was citing Barthes's famous *Camera Lucida* (1981), a keystone text on the subject of picture taking. This photo of Barthes's mother as a child taught him something profound about loss, and it evinced the power of photography in conveying the ineffable through a visual medium. Specifically, in that moment Barthes understood how every photograph is a memorial, bringing back into life someone (or something) who is dead or who has passed out of view.

Dyer's article (2017) was accompanied by a photograph of a himself as a child along with his parents during a family outing in Gloucestershire, England. This photo when Dyer was a boy of approximately the same age as me when I got lost became a stand-in for the missing snapshot of my own family outing at Bear Mountain. Earlier in the column, Dyer describes himself as "the grumpy little fella in the cowboy hat" (p. 14). He takes issue with Barthes's assertion that the terrible fact of every photograph is its containment of the "return of the dead" (p. 14). Dyer doesn't disagree with the assertion itself but with Barthes's view that it is terrible. Dyer speaks for all children about the inevitability of death when he writes:

> The little cowboy doesn't know that yet – how could he when he has not seen this picture? – but he will. Maybe he seems sad because to gaze into the camera is to look into the future. He knows I'll be dead soon.

Of course, this is not something the boy knows but rather something the man knows and is now projecting onto the boy. And even then, the man doesn't fully know what he knows. We look toward both photography and psychoanalysis for a way of understanding what is not readily knowable. I am strangely comforted when I think of "the little cowboy" and the small boy that I was who had temporarily lost his family. That loss portended the subsequent deaths of my parents – my father's when I was a teenager and my mother's 30 years later. And my substitute snapshot documents that we were all there on the day I was lost and found.

Various psychological studies suggest that taking pictures (without focusing in on details) does not improve the memory of what is photographed but also may significantly blur the recollection of what was "shot" by the camera (Henkel, 2014; Hyman, 2013). But while people take photographs to remember actual events (whether it actually aids their memory or not), they also use a camera to remember certain emotions. And the subsequent review of those images helps to fix the emotion in the mind. A photo must be looked at, examined, taken in, mixed in with the viewer's sensibilities, allowed the opportunity to have an effect, and allowed to prick the view like the "punctum" that Barthes describes in *Camera Lucida*. A punctum is a small distinct point, and it is also the term used for the opening of a tear duct. It punctuates. For Barthes, punctum refers to being indelibly touched by a poignant detail. This feels entirely right to me – that looking deeply at a photo of a person – similar to being with and listening to a patient – can get a person to a recognizable place that will make them cry. What is it about art (and music and dance and sports) and psychoanalysis that is so disturbingly emotive?

MY ANALYST, PAUL LIPPMANN

In the photograph of my analyst, from which I derive pleasure, he is surrounded by and embedded in the objects around him. A Royal typewriter is prominently displayed in between two stacks of folders, journals, and newspapers. On a low wooden bookcase against the wall is *The Standard Edition of the Complete Psychological Works of Sigmund Freud*. Twenty-four volumes compose the full standard edition, but I count only 15 on the shelf. Where are the other nine? Are they being used elsewhere for research, to write a paper or book? Were some of the volumes lent out to colleagues or patients? Were the missing volumes never purchased? Was he cheated out of the missing nine? Or are they lost like the child who loses his family? There are also images of people, some of photographs, others drawings or paintings.

On the floor behind him to his right is a framed Norman Rockwell painting, "Girl at the Mirror," in which Rockwell captures the poignancy and uncertainty of adolescence. The props in the painting are a (discarded?) doll, a hair brush and comb, an open lipstick, and a magazine on the girl's lap featuring a picture of Jane Russell, a sexy movie star of the mid-twentieth century. In this moment of transition between childhood and adolescence, the girl and the woman meet and contemplate one another. Juxtaposed with the Rockwell, in the right-hand corner of the painting, is a memorial photo – an image of a woman. She was a beloved member of the Berkshire community where Paul lives (and which had also been home to Norman Rockwell). Because of the depth of field of the camera lens that was used to take the photo, the forefront of the image is somewhat out of focus, but further investigation of this corner of Paul's office leads to the discovery of a second identical memorial photo of the same woman. It is on the middle shelf, positioned between a picture postcard of Gustav Mahler and a smaller photograph of another adolescent girl. The woman's name, Judy Spencer, is on the photo.

What am I looking for in this photograph of my analyst? Having been trained as a photographer and having looked at thousands of photographs – in museums, galleries, magazines, and books, in workshop critiques, under my own loupes, now often as digital files on my computer – I look at each with care and attention to my own responses. The art critic Martin Herbert, when writing about Barthes's *Camera Lucida*, said, "I don't go looking for 'ideas about photography' in that book;

Paul Lippmann, Ph.D.
Elm Street
Stockbridge, Massachusetts
November 20, 2011

I read it for a certain kind of vulnerability" (Dillon, 2011). So like Herbert, I too am looking for vulnerability – in the image of my analyst, standing upright with a slight tilt that raises his left shoulder and results in a faint incline of his head. His enigmatic look strikes me as playful yet deeply penetrating. His right hand covers his left and as they grip each other. I experience a strength that can hold and not let go. He wears a comfortable sweater and trousers and creates the impression of an artist. In fact, he is an artist and has painted abstract faces of tortured souls in his family history, victims of pogroms and the Holocaust, who scream out from their genocidal purgatory, "I have been." This is the phrase Barthes uses to describe the essence of what is found in looking at a photograph. Barthes says, "The Photograph does not call up the past. . . . The effect it produces . . . is not to restore what has been abolished . . . but to attest that what I see has indeed existed" (p. 82).

So when I look at the photographic portrait of my analyst, I see him holding in his hands his therapeutic patients and artistic subjects, and I feel inspired in my journey to bring photography and psychoanalysis into deep conversation, to hold these two passions in my own hands. I am also looking, when I look at him, for vulnerability in myself. Can I see as a means to remember, to attest to the presence of my own existence?

THE PHOTOS IN *AUSTERLITZ*

As with Barthes, who looked at photographs to remember his recently deceased mother, the protagonist in the remarkable novel *Austerlitz* by W. G. Sebald (2001) uses photographs to recover and confirm lost experience. The title character, Jacques Austerlitz, is a small child when he is sent alone from Prague to England on the *Kindertransport* in the summer of 1939. He is told nothing of his Jewish family by the severe, childless couple in Wales who take him in, and although he was sent away from Central Europe and the Nazis for his own safety, his memory of his early childhood vanishes, and he is left with a pervasive and haunting sense of rejection and annihilation. As an adult, fleeting memories begin to pierce his amnesia, and he follows an intense pull beckoning him to retrieve his past from oblivion. The book reads more like a dream than the seemingly straightforward narrative I have presented. The book has no chapters or paragraph breaks, and an anonymous narrator is the recipient and transmitter of Austerlitz's story. Despite its being a work of fiction, *Austerlitz* contains numerous photographs, whose presence conflate the real and the imagined, creating an intermediate state conducive to psychoanalytic exploration. The use of photographic images in *Austerlitz* serves multiple purposes: they illustrate and accompany the text and are in conversation with the story as it evolves, from what seems like an architectural history of train stations and municipal buildings in Europe to a poignant quest to recover a lost past. The photos are also repeating patterns mirroring memory itself, and they inspire the idea that photographs search out people and inquire into their unconscious associations and involuntary memories.

LOOKING IN PSYCHOANALYSIS

This understanding of photographic imagery as catalyzing repressed or dissociated memory and bringing it into an available consciousness is found in the visual presence of the psychoanalytic office – if one is able to see and be seen. When people first come into a psychoanalytic office, they are looking for relief of something painful, for relief from some suffering. In some instances entrance into psychoanalysis comes at the insistence of others in a patient's life. The pressure from spouses, parents, or employers can force someone into psychoanalytic treatment, but to want to stay, the patient must begin to look for something – something that is missing. In his *Introductory Lectures on Psychoanalysis* (1917), Freud describes the task of psychoanalytic therapy as "[filling] all the gaps in the patient's memory, to remove his amnesias" (p. 282), which is the same as his famous dictum of "making the unconscious conscious." The analyst and the photographer may be seen as sharing an intentionality in trying to identify the gaps and use their methods to fill these spaces with new experiences, with new images. This perspective favors what is considered in psychoanalysis as a one-person psychology, and it fails to recognize the inevitability of interaction and mutual influence in the analytic relationship. As a relational analyst and photographer, I am more interested in the jointly constructed experience of photographers (who Barthes disparagingly called "operators") in concert with the subjects of their photographic portraits and of psychoanalysts in relationship with their patients as two parties involved in the project of trying to see and be seen.

In the very first meeting of a potential patient and potential psychoanalyst (because being a psychoanalyst always requires the participation and agreement of an analysand), something extraordinary happens in the time it would take to click the shutter of a camera. Each person gets a glimpse of the other in an initial encounter that can shape all that will follow. In an interesting article on the therapist's body, Jane Burka (2001), in writing about her experience as an overweight therapist, says, "I am overweight, in the heavy/*zoftig*/earth mother range and my shape is sometimes an explicit subject of exploration with my patients" (p. 255). She describes a first session with a prospective patient who tells her toward the end of the hour that she has decided not to work with her. After giving some reasons that seem suspect, Burka inquires what else might have influenced her decision. The woman admits that it is the therapist's weight that feels too risky. Burka goes on to point to the ignoring of the (therapist) body in the professional literature and by extension to disregarding the body in psychoanalysis. This oversight applies to both parties in the psychoanalytic encounter and continues throughout treatment. It also pertains to other physical and visual aspects of the person's face, dress, gestures, and objects and decor of the office. Yet "checking each other out," or responding to a person's physical presence, is taking place at different levels of consciousness and at all times. What is the reluctance to acknowledge this mutual eyeing of each other?

We have all been acculturated to a greater or lesser extent with the prohibition against staring ("It's not polite!"). Patients are often exquisitely attuned to their analysts' vulnerabilities and to the hierarchical need for compliance (Burka, 2001). Looking at one another in a very attended way can also generate deeply held anxieties of sexual violation. And to look with a penetrating gaze is to risk seeing beneath the mask that we all need to present of ourselves. What we see may disturb and frighten us about the other and what it in turn reflects about ourselves.

If we accept that psychoanalysis in its many guises has some basic core understandings (i.e., that the mind and its effects are far more unconscious than conscious and that transference and countertransference are the primary means of human communication), then it can be argued, as we have already touched on in Chapter 1, that there is a long unbroken tradition from Freud's office to any other psychoanalytic office in any location, right up to the present. In other words, it follows that the essence of psychoanalysis – its core presuppositions – must permeate, in the shadowy confines of unconscious space, all the offices that have descended from Bergasse 19. Yet it is undeniable that psychoanalysis has grown, and must continue to grow, by its exchanges with advances in knowledge and the challenges of diversity to its localized and incestuous origins. The notion of the gaze, how it has evolved, and what is available to see in the psychoanalytic office are areas where therapists can extend their understanding.

There is a long, controversial history in psychoanalysis about the arrangement of the office, particularly regarding the placement and use of the couch and the analyst's chair. Freud (1913, p. 133) had a personal reason for his insistence on the procedure "of getting the patient to lie on the sofa while I sit behind him out of his sight," which was because he could not tolerate being stared at by others for many hours a day. Thomas Ogden (1994) justified and elaborated on Freud's reason for this approach by emphasizing that it facilitates the conditions for both analysand and analyst to engage in a reverie state that connects to the unconscious "third" produced by the meeting of two minds. The third is the essence of psychoanalysis, Ogden argued. In my view the idea of staying out of each other's sight is an illusion. We see even if we insist on our blindness. This is true whatever arrangements are found and used in the room with whatever furnishings are available.

Looking at the other steadily, intently, and with fixed attention is the definition of the verb "gaze." Psychoanalysts have been interested in this activity since Freud first drew attention to scopophilia (1913), or deriving of pleasure from looking. For Freud, this was a natural activity expressing sexuality that is found in childhood, and over time the gaze can be sublimated in an interest in art or in looking at beautiful images. Alternately, scopophilia can become a perversion when it morphs into an exclusive sexual pleasure, a voyeurism in looking at nakedness, the sexual activities of others, and/or pornography. The reverse perverse position is exhibitionism, the pleasure of being the recipient of the gaze of the other. For Freud, these perversions came at the cost of being able to develop a mature sexual relationship with another adult.

The French psychoanalyst Jacques Lacan (1964) brought an additional understanding to the experience of the gaze, which is the notion that in the anxious realization that if you, as subject, can gaze upon the other, then there is another subject who exists who can gaze at you. The object of our eyes' look is somehow looking back at us of its own will. There is no safety in the gaze; rather, it contains the existential awareness that looking challenges the illusion of privacy and makes us face our essential lack of control and potential for exposure.

My project of photographing analysts in their offices is based on my interest in the conundrum of what can be disclosed in psychoanalysis. This issue of disclosure–exposure is often a central concern of analysts. Contemporary analysts understand that analytic anonymity is a fiction (Singer, 1977/2017) and that use of the self (Jacobs, 1991; Kuchuck, 2014) is an essential tool in treatment. But alternately there is great concern about the analyst's capacity to violate the patient's sense of safety (Dimen, 2011). The anxiety generated by this dilemma is one important reason the profession keeps itself relatively out of the limelight, but in so doing it mystifies itself as well as the public. I am interested in understanding my own profession better and in opening up the office in which we practice in an effort to make this "impossible profession" (Malcolm, 1982) a bit more transparent. As I myself look, I realize I become more seen, and this experience can be equally exciting and disturbing. Growth and self-knowledge are rarely acts of volition. But while they confuse and disorganize the status quo, they also provide an enlivened space for both patient and analyst.

The concept of the "male gaze" was first coined by the British film theorist Laura Mulvey (1999), who used Freudian and Lacanian psychoanalytic theory to critique the oppression of women in a phallocentric order. Mulvey shows how movies demonstrate the patriarchal system, with its gendered division involving pleasure. The male creator and spectator derive the benefits of the female actress/model's provision of her sexuality for their satisfaction and viewing pleasure (Mulvey, 1999). Moreover, the male gaze also applies to male analysts working with female patients. More recent works of analysts, influenced by feminist, queer, and diversity orientations (Stack, 1999) and by maternal–infant research (Beebe, Cohen, & Lachmann, 2016) have evolved ideas about the gaze from nontraditional viewpoints, extending the concept to the female gaze, the maternal gaze, and the outsider gaze. Clinical examples from my own practice exemplify the challenges and rewards of using the gaze as a way to see what often is blind in the psychoanalytic office. One such case involved someone with expertise in photography.

TWO PATIENTS: KATIE AND JOANNA

Katie entered the room, taking it all in as she rotated her head and gave 360-degree attention to the walls. When she sat down, she looked at me closely as though deciding how much of herself was possible to show. I asked her what she saw of my office and what impressions she had. After pausing for a moment she said, "All those diplomas on the wall have your back." I had been expecting her to comment on the framed photograph on the wall above my head as other patients usually do. It is titled *Voyagers Horizon* and shows a calm ocean view at sundown in mostly orange tones. The photograph appears to be from the perspective of someone in the ocean, probably on a boat, and has an abstract quality to it, like a painting – a study in orange, from light peach through grayish brown. It's a piece of art I like, and I am comfortable with what it might say about me. Buying it early in my career, I was drawn to the photo in part because it did not reveal much about my personal self.

By contrast, Katie's comment caught me by surprise. I rarely think about the five diplomas that hang on the wall vertically over my left shoulder: my diplomas from graduate school, my postdoctoral certificate attesting to my completion of training in psychoanalysis, and the state license that demonstrates my lawful practice as a psychologist. I am proud of the accomplishments these diplomas represent, and I do believe that people seeking psychotherapy have a right to know the person they are seeing has been properly trained and vetted to practice. But in this initial moment with Katie, I felt as if she had seen through me. These documents hanging on my wall "had my back." They concealed an anxious concern before meeting a new patient, that I would not be up for the task, that I was not sufficiently educated, had not trained enough, had not read as extensively as I should have. She saw that they were shoring me up.

My first impression of Katie was complicated by my knowing that she was a writer and had written on the subjects of art and photography. I was excited by the prospect of working with someone with interests similar to mine, but I was also slightly intimidated. I was approaching the session with curiosity but not dispassion. I studied her face like a portrait painting or photograph and saw tension and hesitancy. Her mouth seemed to be holding anxiety. She was holding back tears. I felt connected to her struggle, and as we talked in that first session, she cried. Had she seen the uncried tears in my eyes, as I recognized her faltering efforts to maintain a mask of stoic control? She told me of a photographer whose work she found interesting, especially a project in which this man had photographed himself in his father's clothing. She thought about how she represented herself and how she was good at looking. In addition to her demonstrable skill at gazing, I also found her good-looking, and this made me uncomfortable, as I sensed that she would be able to see me in ways in which I would not be sufficiently aware. Over time I learned that we shared an interest in self-portraiture. I began my project of photographing analysts in their offices by photographing myself, trying to see what others saw of me in this place. My curiosity about what other analysts will look like in my photographs is partially based on an embarrassing need to see myself.

I have a number of my photographs hanging in my office:

- a narrow winding street in Florence, Italy, that leads into the Piazza del Duomo, which in the picture is just a slit of light in the diminishing distance;
- an inside shot of La Grupa Hot Springs in San Miguel de Allende in Mexico, a stone-domed tunnel of steamy, chest-deep water, whose walls close in on a darkened terminus in the center of the photo; and

• the empty seats at La Bombonera in Buenos Aires, the home stadium of the Boca Juniors football team, where the visual lines in the photograph from the low perspective of the camera go off into what seems infinite space.

I had always conceived of these images as reflective of the uncertain journey of psychoanalysis, but when Katie dialed her keenly observant eye upon them, she called them voids, vaginal passages. I thought at the time that she was on to something unconscious in me and important in our psychoanalytic relationship. She would not relinquish the gaze to me, and in her insistence to have her own view, established a place where there could be more freedom to see each other and ourselves.

If men can see themselves as containing a wound or lack, or of being in a position of need, and if that view of themselves does not obliterate the more admirable masculine qualities of courage and honor, then the possibilities for more varied and freer relational configurations can be experienced to the benefit of both members of a psychoanalytic couple. In a discussion that mirrors this stance, Jessica Benjamin (2004) uses film theorist Kaja Silverman's illustration of the World War II film *The Best Years of Our Lives*. The movie depicts the emotionally and physically traumatized veterans returning from mortal combat, including the actor Harold Russell, who lost both his hands in a bomb explosion and had two hooks in place of the missing extremities.

Benjamin (2004) says of these men that "the film shows how their wounding and symbolic castration results in a kind of reversal, in which women now gaze upon the spectacle of male lack. This spectacle is erotized, but not as humiliation" (p. 54).

During a difficult time in my life, in which my freedom to see and be seen was enhanced by my own vulnerability, I worked with another patient, Joanna, who sobbed deeply and for long periods. She expressed a feeling that everything was falling apart, which I attributed to her aloneness in the world, the damaging influence of early family disruption, the dangerous allure of sexuality, and a feeling of hopelessness about ever being in a long-term, loving, and trusting relationship with a man. In retrospect, it appears so clear to me that she was also referencing how I was falling apart. For months I had been conducting sessions while I was experiencing persistent aching pain in my lower back, hips, upper legs, and knees. I could not find a comfortable position anywhere. On a number of occasions, I had to stand up with patients, explaining as I did that I had some back pain. Although I strove to be available, I could not tolerate too much attention to my body, which felt inhabited by alien forces intent on torturing me.

During one session on the day of a torrential rainstorm, Joanna had started crying shortly after the session began, and her cries escalated to sobs as she reported that the leaks in her apartment were still not fixed and she hated being there, a place in which she lived alone. At times like this she feared her status as single and uncoupled would never change. I shifted uncomfortably in my seat, unable to find a position that could contain Joanna's anguish and my own terrible pain. She had been witness to my pain and saw how my body and the body of our work that held us afloat in the turbulence of her analysis were leaking badly and threatening to destroy all of the progress of the safe voyage we had thus far traveled.

Eventually the pain I was experiencing reached a level I could no longer endure. Following an MRI and the discovery of an unusual tumor at the base of my spine, surgery became the only option. The surgery, described as a "radical approach," involved a team of surgeons working ten hours in the operating room to remove the tumor while preserving the integrity of my spinal cord. There was a second surgery five days later that inserted a metal plate where part of my lumbar vertebrae had been removed. Once sufficiently recovered from the surgeries to my abdomen and back, I had seven weeks of daily targeted radiation treatments.

After returning to the office to see Joanna for the first time in months, I realized she was in the bathroom. As I waited for her to enter, I held onto the edge of a credenza and moved my legs into a position to stretch my hamstring muscles. I was still in some pain, but it had been diminishing, and the stretching motion felt good for my body and for my spirit. Joanna was an avid runner who started most mornings with a six-mile course in the park. Through our interactions and her observations, including her attention to two figurines of bicyclists on a shelf in my office, she had correctly assessed that sports and physical activities had a central place in my life. I heard her approaching and decided in a split second that I would not move immediately to my chair but would continue to hold my pose. I was aware that I wanted her to see me being physical, to feel that she was with a strong and flexible man who was fit enough to help her. But there was also something else going on that was shown and being seen. She had told me she was feeling sad and wished the man she was dating was bigger. She said that he was very thin and had no chest hair. I was so aware during this time of the large, disfiguring scars on my back and abdomen and of the weakness and pain I was still experiencing, that the obvious opportunity to explore Joanna's reaction to *my* physical appearance, through her reference to disappointment with this man, completely eluded me until later in the treatment.

As my recovery continued, our work moved forward. Five months after surgery, the radiation treatments had been completed. I was no longer in pain and began to anticipate the coming of spring and my return to the tennis courts. Joanna was also in an anticipatory mood, discussing what it would be like to be with her new boyfriend on the upcoming weekend. She noticed her anxieties, both disturbing and exciting, around having intercourse and experiencing an orgasm. She became self-consciously aware as she pictured herself and this man naked as she was talking with me. She said that it was a very strange feeling to have because she usually felt so comfortable telling me anything. I experienced myself in a privileged position, recognized by this woman as a trusted therapist, as a man, and as someone who was vitally needed and alive. She told me I had been her analyst, a father figure, and a practice boyfriend. I felt that one important marker of my recovery was met by the experience of feeling sexually alive in the presence of another sexually alive person.

I took a selfie years later while in London, and in preparing to dress for it, I self-consciously looked at my body. Then, as now, as I retrieve that image from the photo app on my iPhone, the scars are noticeable. I can look at myself and see the evidence of what I lost. The memory of that difficult time reenters and with it a haunting trace of the pain and fear that accompanied it. But I also remember that time as when Joanna and I could risk being vulnerable in each other's presence, to see and be seen and share the gift of mutual healing.

5 Psychoanalyst as photographic subject

When someone asked the great portrait photographer Annie Leibowitz, "What is a photographer's life?" she responded, "It's just a life . . . working through a lens." I cannot claim a photographer's life of seeing through the camera's lens every day, but I will be forever grateful to Karen Haberberg, who led a portfolio review class I attended, for giving me the confidence to see myself as a photographer. Once a month Haberberg's class met at the Jewish Community Center in Manhattan, with a different composition of participants showing up each time. A few people returned from month to month, and I was one of the regulars. At the start of each meeting, people went around the room introducing themselves. My introduction always began with some variation of "I'm not really a photographer." One day Karen interrupted and challenged my negation of a photographer's identity. I had been showing my work for decades, and after that night it began to dawn on me that perhaps I was a photographer. My primary career identity as a psychoanalyst did not preclude identifying myself as an artist with a camera.

JOYCE MCDOUGALL IN PARIS

In April 2006, I traveled to Paris to photograph analysts. The blush of spring colors in the flowers and foliage and in the clothing of Parisians was a welcome sight, but I did not feel hopeful. I was scheduled to photograph Joyce McDougall, a renowned figure in psychoanalysis. I was in town for a week, for the purpose of making additional connections with analysts in the hope I could get in more than one photoshoot. The trip was challenging because of the pain I had been experiencing in my lower body for almost a month, which escalated on the flight. After takeoff I had to stand in the galley for the remainder of the trip, where I worried about whether I could physically handle the shoots. I was now about three years into my project of photographing analysts and had stopped using only a tripod for the portraits, which meant that photographing became a kind of workout. As I would move about the office of the analyst with my camera, always looking for the image, I would bend my knees, stand on my toes, lie on the floor, scrunch up for a closeup, and push back against the far wall to get more of the room in the frame. I was concerned that my body would not allow for the necessary flexibility demanded for the task.

Kimberly Leary, Ph.D.
Massachusetts Avenue
Cambridge, Massachusetts
September 21, 2004

Accompanying me was an assistant, a recent New York University graduate of photography and digital imaging. Originally from Israel, Shiri and I had forged a good working relationship. She assisted me on the first shoots in New York and then accompanied me to Cambridge, Massachusetts, to photograph Kim Leary and then to northern California, where I photographed six analysts in four days. I felt a little more secure in Paris knowing that this strong young woman would be in the room with me, helping to set up the lights and assisting in numerous other ways.

Joyce McDougall's office was near Les Halles market and not far from Le Marais, a major center of the Parisian Jewish community and LGBTQ culture. Born in New Zealand, McDougall first came to London at age 29 to study psychoanalysis with Anna Freud and Donald Winnicott. She later settled in Paris, where she joined the Paris Psychoanalytic Society and became a student of Jacques Lacan. American analysts first became familiar with her though her work in psychosomatic illness, described in her landmark contribution, *Theatres of the Body* (1989). I was certain when I came to photograph her that spring that I was suffering from just such a psychosomatic illness (proved to have an organic cause a few months later). I considered consulting with her, but our schedules for the week I was in town were not compatible. She was a welcoming and approachable hostess, a vibrant and beautiful presence in her high-ceilinged office filled with art. The subject herself was accompanied by her beloved dog Giselle.

Joyce McDougall was that rare analyst who built a strong foundation on a number of competing psychoanalytic theories. Clinically gifted, she possessed a liveliness that when encountered made the person in front of her feel more human. She wrote that "each person in his psychic complexity is a masterpiece," and the title of her first major book, *Plea for a Measure of Abnormality* (1992), expressed her belief in the dignity of all people. Anthony Molino (1997) captures her warmth and eccentricity in a description of an international call she made to him at 3 a.m., when they when they were in the process of arranging an interview:

By the time we'd finalized the arrangements for our interview and, like people meeting on a blind date, got down to the business of determining just how we'd manage to recognize each other, "Joyce" then put the finishing touch on a wonderfully wacky call: "I'll be the woman with the rose in her mouth!"

(Molino, 1997, p. 53)

During our photoshoot in 2006, she told me a joke that made me laugh deeply, so that I temporarily forgot my physical suffering. Within the context of discussing the psychoanalytic frame or "rules," she quipped:

A long analysis was close to termination, and the patient asked if at the end he could kiss his analyst. "No," she replied, strictly enforcing the code of analytic abstinence. Later the patient asked if it would be permissible for the analyst to kiss him. "No," she said, "that is not what we are here for." The patient persisted

Joyce McDougall, Ed.D.
Rue Quincampoix
Paris, France
April 13, 2006

in this line of questioning until the analyst finally said, "Please stop asking. It's bad enough I'm lying on the couch with you."

When I reviewed my correspondence with McDougall after I returned to New York, I was surprised to discover I had shot her one week before her 86th birthday; she seemed so vibrant and youthful. She was gracious even before I met her in person, inviting me in the previous year to visit her in Spain if I happened to be there where she was vacationing. When Shiri and I were packing up after the photoshoot, Joyce handed me a book – a memoir by her late second husband, Sidney Stewart, an American who had settled in France in 1948 to study psychoanalysis. A survivor of the Bataan death march in the Philippines and three years in Japanese captivity during the World War II, he wrote *Give Us This Day* (1986), an account of how prisoners endured their suffering. He shared with McDougall an interest in psychic survival in extreme circumstances, as well as an interest in the nature of creativity.

Joyce connected me with her friend and colleague Genevieve Welsh, whom I also photographed in Paris and who kindly hosted a dinner party with her family and other psychoanalysts on the occasion of my visit. I continued to periodically exchange emails with Genevieve, who informed me when Joyce's dog Giselle died and later when Joyce herself died at 91. Because I had spent such pleasurable time in her company, I missed her. In her interview with Molino, Joyce described the differences between two seminal thinkers in psychoanalysis who both influenced her – Donald Winnicott and Jacques Lacan:

Lacan favored splits and divisions . . . whereas Winnicott was always trying to bring groups to understand each other and work together. Winnicott believed that you had to work at creating a containing space in which people would feel safe and slowly develop a sense of trust. Lacan on the contrary warned that the patient must never feel at ease; and should be under constant pressure.

(Molino, 1997, pp. 63–64)

Lacan's analytic technique included determining when each session ended, whether at five minutes or more, keeping the patient in a heightened state of active anxiety. Winnicott, the British pediatrician turned psychoanalyst, created a holding environment to contain the splits in selfhood. The Winnicottian analyst in the clinical setting has been likened to a "good-enough mother." It seemed clear to me that Joyce was more in tune with Winnicott's love than with Lacan's manipulations. I am grateful that I got to meet Joyce McDougall while she was still healthy and spirited with love and play. The psychoanalytic scholar Peter Rudnytsky, upon seeing my portrait of Joyce at an exhibition, wrote to me, "The only time I met Joyce was last year in London. She was a shadow of her former elegant self, which you captured so beautifully" (personal communication, March 3, 2012).

Genevieve Welsh, MD
Rue Fagon
Paris, France
April 20, 2006

ANDRE GREEN AND INTIMATIONS OF THE DEAD MOTHER

Both McDougall and her "good friend" Andre Green had attended Lacan's famous lectures in Paris, which she had described as a very inspiring period in her life. She had been taken with Lacan's brilliance as a theorist but felt that the way he worked clinically was sometimes an excuse for his own idiosyncrasies. Green was also impressed with Lacan's intelligence and appreciated the resurgence of interest in Freud in France, which Lacan championed. Green was close with Lacan for a number of years but then broke with him over the latter's position that the unconscious is formed in the way that language is acquired and ignoring the sexual drives. Lacan's psychoanalysis remained intellectual, according to Green, and he misused his celebrity status in treating patients. Green said:

> In the analytic situation he [Lacan] became a kind of Zen master, doing absolutely anything he wanted, not following any rule. . . . He talks of the Name-of-the-Father as a theoretical reference, but in fact he behaves more like an abusive mother than a law-providing father.

(Benvenuto, 1995–96)

Through an introduction from Joyce McDougall, I had the opportunity to meet and photograph Andre Green in his office in Paris in 2006. Like McDougall, Green arrived in Paris from somewhere else. In his case, he came to Europe from Egypt at age 19 to study medicine. Green's body of work has been influential in the psychoanalytic world, especially in France, Europe, and Latin America, and has gradually had an impact on North American psychoanalysis. At the time of our meeting and photoshoot, I knew only that Green was a reputed classical Freudian analyst, and I associated him with his most well-known concept, "the dead mother." Green (1983) described the dead mother as:

> an (image) which has been constituted in the child's mind, following maternal depression, brutally transforming a living object, which was a source of vitality for the child, into a distant figure, toneless, practically inanimate. . . . The dead mother . . . is a mother who remains alive but who is, so to speak, psychically dead in the eyes of the young child in her care.

(p. 142)

In an interview by Gregorio Kohon (1999), Green explained his personal interest in this subject:

> . . . my mother had a depression: she had a younger sister, who died after being burned accidentally. She was the youngest sister of the family, my Aunt Rose, and my mother got depressed. I have seen photographs – one can tell from her face that she had really a very severe depression. . . . I can only suppose that I have been very strongly marked by this experience.

(p. 14)

As it turned out, the experience of photographing Andre Green felt like being in a classical analytic session with a dead mother in the room. His office was attractively decorated, yet I felt a certain coldness in the air. There was a large wooden sculpture above his chair, which I later learned he had found in Brazil and thought might be a rendering of Joseph or Jesus. In retrospect, it was an interesting *objet d'art* for a secular Jew, a self-described *apatride* (stateless person), who criticized Lacan for rewriting Freud's psychoanalysis in a Christian key (Benvenuto, 1995). Although I was a practicing psychoanalyst and a chronologically mature adult, I immediately felt subordinate in his office. He sat very motionless in his chair, showing little in body language or facial expression. When I asked him, "How do you prepare to listen?" he replied, "In the least possible way." I began to feel like a patient and as if he were my distant, toneless, practically inanimate analyst.

My Uncle Paul, a physician, married a woman who had been a nun when they met during his medical training. After they fell in love, she left the order and in time became my Aunt Marian. Hanging on the wall in their home was a large crucifix of a bloody Jesus nailed to the cross, with a look of deep suffering on his face. I was always scared in the presence of that object, the specter of painful death in atonement for human transgression. In retrospect, I wonder if Andre Green's Jesus and my own physical suffering during this period had joined with his "dead mother" and the memory of my aunt's suffering Jesus to co-create my odd experience in his office. After finishing a roll of color film on my Mamiya RZ 67, I suggested we take a break while I, with the help of Shiri, prepared the next camera, my Nikon, with a roll of black-and-white film. I was relieved to not be in such intense contact with Green, who remained implacably stiff in his analyst's chair with his back toward me.

I had been addressing him as Dr. Green, which was not entirely a reflection of appropriate politeness. Rather, I felt under a constant pressure, like I imagined a patient might feel in Lacanian analysis. Once the camera was loaded and we were ready to resume, I wanted to get Green's attention. Something unbidden arose in me, and I called out, "Andre!" He turned, and I clicked the shutter, resuming the photoshoot. When I returned to New York and perused the contact sheets, I began the process of looking for the one image that would do justice to the experience of being with him in his office. All of the color images were technically sound, but they lacked vitality. It was that first shot of unpreparedness for us both that felt right – the one I snapped after I called out "Andre." Green's terse comment about preparing "in the least possible way" proved prescient and wise. There was also something about the image being in black and white that was compatible with his contributions to psychoanalytic thinking about all forms of loss. For Green, severe depression is colored black, while the rest if life is a blankness or white-colored state of emptiness.

Andre Green, MD
Avenue de l'Observatoire
Paris, France
April 24, 2006

THE OFFICE AND ANALYST AS ENVIRONMENTAL PORTRAIT

All my portraits of psychoanalysts in their offices are, by definition, environmental portraits. An environmental portrait is one executed in the subject's usual environment, such as in their home or workplace, and it typically illuminates the subject's life and surroundings. Two masters of this genre who have energized my work are Arnold Newman and Alfred Eisenstaedt. Newman explains his approach to the environmental portrait as follows:

> I don't just want to make a photograph with some things in the background. The surroundings had to add to the composition and the understanding of the person. No matter who the subject was, it has to be an interesting photograph. Just to do a portrait of a famous person doesn't mean a thing.
>
> (M. E. Harris, 2000, p. 37)

Eisenstaedt preferred small 35-mm cameras like the Leica M over the more bulky 4×5 Press Cameras with flash attachments popular into the mid-twentieth century. He felt this created a more relaxed mood with his subjects and said, "They don't take me too seriously with my little camera. I don't come as a photographer. I come as a friend" (Goldberg, 1986, p. 80). Greatly influenced by the psychoanalytic orientation of seeing mutual inspiration in the creation of any new experience, I have aspired to the beautifully constructed works of Newman and the we-are-in-this-together modesty of Eisenstaedt in creating my own style.

Working with assistants has greatly improved and inspired my work. Most are photographers, trained in photography and the arts. Their technical skills, especially in the area of lighting, have been superior to my own. But in addition, there is a dynamic when a third person is in the room in a portrait photoshoot. The permutations of interpersonal and intrapsychic dynamics increase exponentially. I have not always had the luxury of an assistant on my shoots. In some instances, I have contacted a psychoanalyst in a region in which I was traveling through for a vacation or a conference without much planning or advance notice, and for those shoots I worked alone. But in contrast to Alfred Eisenstaedt, who famously said he preferred working alone and that he wished the camera could operate even without him, I welcome another person in the space I am visiting with the analyst. I find that the anxiety of the intensity of the experience of this intimate encounter is contained within a third presence and that a transitional space can be found more extemporaneously, which can help create a realized image.

IMPROVISATION INSPIRED BY PHILLIP RINGSTROM

In 2014, my son Ben, a musician and sometime videographer, accompanied me as assistant on a photoshoot of Phillip Ringstrom. Ben and I were on a road trip down the California coast during a transitional period in his life. We had started in San Francisco, where he was living, and meandered south with a planned stop in Encino to photograph Ringstrom. I had not been in Encino for many years, the city where I had been a patient in therapy while living in southern California in the 1970s. My therapist at the time had subsequently retired to an island off the coast of Washington state. Not having been able to locate him with a Google search and calculating that he would be close to 100, I felt a sense of loss as we entered Encino. I had also been telling Ben of the wonderful food I remembered from my days in Ventura County. The previous day we had stopped at Otani's, a Japanese fish market in Oxnard, where I would often eat red snapper teriyaki for lunch. But the food didn't taste the same, and I was aware of the sadness of losing something important from the past, since the food was associated with a time in my youth long gone.

Philip Ringstrom seemed the perfect subject while I was in this mood, since he is an important contributor to contemporary relational psychoanalysis. Some shoots are more enjoyable than others, and photographing Phil was great fun. Spending time with him was like participating in the improvisational theatre he uses as a metaphor for a more authentic psychoanalytic experience, one that can involve reverie, play, and spontaneous engagement. "Although such moments arise unpredictably," says Ringstrom, "they capture something of both the analyst's and the analysand's fundamental personality organizations." He continues, saying,

> These are represented in how each one's experience of the *past, present*, and *future* are organized in "scriptlike" manners. The improvisational interplay of their "scripts" lend themselves to "scenes" from which a co-constructed *relational unconscious* emerges, that is, a quality of "thirdness" that neither can lay exclusive claim to authoring.
>
> (Ringstrom, 2007, p. 69)

We initially met Phil at his house and then followed him a few blocks to another house he used exclusively as his office. I felt as if this office was his own playhouse, a personal community theater to which he invited another or others, and each would bring their scripts and create scenes that could lead to riffing among the participants' unconscious minds. Phil is a high-energy person with a quick mind that lends itself to improvisation and humor. Ben is also verbally acute, and his years of playing in bands have honed a natural talent for performing as part of a system. I felt freer in the room with these two high-energy guys to find my own "seens." The three of us were having fun as I was framing images and considering lighting conditions and focusing. At some point, Phil went to his couch, and I shot and shot and shot. I felt his aliveness entering the lens, buoying me and releasing some of the sadness that had come down the coast for the ride.

When Ben and I left Phil's playhouse, I felt emboldened to attempt to find another beloved food haunt from those days gone by. Across from my old therapist's office on Ventura Boulevard, not far from where the photoshoot had taken place, had been Du-par's Restaurant. It was already iconic in the 1970s, having been established in 1938. Their pancakes were the best I ever ate. The heightened

Phil Ringstrom, Ph.D., Psy.D.
Haskell Avenue
Encino, California
February 15, 2014

mood triggered by being with Phil in his office was dissolved when we discovered that Du-par's Encino no longer existed. However, there was a Du-par's in Studio City, and we arrived at the restaurant the next morning. The waitresses wore the same old-timey uniforms with aprons, and the waiters had the same vests. When the pancakes arrived, they were as fluffy as I remembered them, and on the side of the plate were the two familiar small containers, one holding warm maple syrup and the other melted butter. The first taste proved these were the same pancakes I had eaten in 1970. I was suffused with a feeling of contentment, as something of the past came alive again. Here I was sitting with my son, eating the best pancakes in the world, on the spot where Mack Sennett filmed his silent movie comedies, the Keystone Kops films, beginning in 1928 in Studio City. The sweet warmth of the food, the familial closeness, and the improvisational moments with Phil Ringstrom in his office theater held me in an embrace. In that moment I felt myself to be entirely living the life of a photographer.

Gallery A

Velleda Ceccoli, Ph.D.
West 58th Street
New York, New York
October 7, 2013

Otto Kernberg, MD
West 42nd Street
New York, New York
December 22, 2017

Erin Mullin, Ph.D.
Divisadero Street
San Francisco, California
February 27, 2004

Susie Orbach, Ph.D.
Lancaster Drive
London, England
August 9, 2005

Sam Gerson, Ph.D.
Fillmore Street
San Francisco, California
November 23, 2016

Eyal Rozmarin, Ph.D.
Lafayette Street
New York, New York
September 30, 2004

Kirkland Vaughans, Ph.D.
Broadway
New York, New York
February 11, 2006

Tracy Simon, Ph.D.
Lafayette Street
New York, New York
July 29, 2011

Ted Jacobs, MD
East 87th Street
New York, New York
May 27, 2016

Leanh Nguyen, Ph.D.
2nd Avenue
New York, New York
January 22, 2005

6   The image in psychoanalysis

I have often had the thought that seeing – not English – is my first language. Becoming a photographer, and even a psychoanalyst, has been rooted in this primary capacity to know and relate to the world, and images were my first vocabulary. I can still picture the view out the window looking onto the firehouse across the street from my first childhood home. A small bookcase that my father built I can readily visualize, with its graduated steps on one side that I could sit upon and the shelves containing my and my sister's books and toys. Although never formally trained and not especially talented, I have sketched and drawn the world since my early childhood. I stuttered as a boy and saw a speech therapist in elementary school. The part of the speech therapy I most remember is looking at myself in the mirror, practicing exercises of using my tongue to try to touch my nose, then my chin, and then forming it into a hot dog roll. These evocative images connect me to the visual and sensual parts of my childhood, the shame of having trouble speaking, and the shy gratitude to that now anonymous speech therapist for helping me learn to communicate more comfortably.

Patients too have told me of their recollections of very early images and other emotionally charged sensory experiences. A man who was given up at birth and then adopted shortly thereafter as an infant claims to remember the strange smell of his new home, which he associates with the image of his adoptive mother. He says he must have felt anxiety about being in the wrong house with the wrong mother. Multisensory environments are routinely employed for individuals previously isolated by their perceptual disabilities. There is also evidence that multisensory experience aids in learning and retention (Shams & Seitz, 2008). Psychoanalysis can be thought of as a complex learning experience involving emotional, cognitive, and behavioral domains. In this analogy to learning, the task is to unlearn or relearn the unfulfilling and destructive relationally held patterns that are maintained outside of awareness.

THE VISUAL FIELD IN THE PSYCHOANALYST'S OFFICE

Seeing is but one dimension of the multisensory experience contained in the patient's encounter with the analyst and their room, but the importance of this meeting frequently has been overlooked. The visual field in this concurrence includes the physical existence and appearance of analyst and patient and the object-filled space in which analysis takes place. What surrounds and faces analysts, as they sit in their offices, are essential components of finding and generating evocative imagery for psychoanalytic work. These are images that summon emotional responses, as when a photograph from the past brings tears to one's eyes. If the visual field is overlooked or minimized, great swaths of significant, complex, and often problematic relational experience can become blind spots in the therapy. My approach to imagery, informed by my work as both photographer and psychoanalyst, emphasizes appearance and absence. In previous discussions of the spaces and objects in psychoanalytic offices (Gerald, 2011, 2015), I have viewed these rooms as holding environments for the creative potential of psychoanalytic action. The images and vast imaginative possibilities in these offices are in us as much as we are in their imagistic space.

Since Freud's time, psychoanalysis has privileged hearing over seeing and thinking over feeling. In her book on how rooms and writers shape one another, Diana Fuss (2004) emphasizes the affective qualities of architectural spaces. Her chapter "Bergasse 19, Vienna Austria" (Fuss & Sanders, 2004), Sigmund Freud's office and home for almost 50 years, is a fascinating and detailed account of the dimensions, windows, doorways, furnishings, and objects inside and of the spatial context of the neighborhood and world in which this first psychoanalytic office existed. As mentioned in Chapter 1, the death of Freud's father greatly influenced the physical existence and experience of this iconic space, one that still reverberates in all subsequent analytic offices.

According to Fuss and Sanders, Freud created "an overdetermined space of loss and absence, grief and memory, elegy and mourning, . . . [Patients] entered the exteriorized theater of Freud's own emotional history, where every object newly found memorialized a love-object lost" (p. 79). The arrangements of the furnishings in the Bergasse 19 space, particularly the couch and analyst's chair, facilitate "an erotics of voice, privileging sound over sight, speech over spectatorship" (2004, p. 94), say Fuss and Sanders. As such, the space emphasizes talking as cure. Along with this were prohibitions against using the body, including the eyes:

> While doctor and patient are located on the same side of the window, the patient alone is visually empowered while Freud is functionally blinded. Freud can listen but he cannot see; hearing must compensate for a radical loss of vision. Once again then, Freud imagines himself as a passive, responsive organ.
>
> (Fuss & Sanders, 2004, p. 96)

Have analysts been blind to what is right before their eyes? The Oedipus myth, so central in psychoanalysis, teaches that blindness (self-inflicted) is the punishment for crossing certain boundaries. This consequence of diminished sensory capacity has been understood primarily as a guilt-induced reaction for killing the father and desiring the mother (Freud, 1930) or, alternatively, as a shame-based response to failure (Kilborne, 2002). Patients and analysts must adhere to the frame of self-restraint. This is required even when the audacity of seeing and the recognition of that freedom can better fit the picture of the patient and the analyst (Bass, 2007). Although Freud did not have as rigid a frame as some Freudians who followed him, the rules of psychoanalysis in his name became sacrosanct in keeping the analyst anonymous, neutral, non-gratifying, and often blind to their contribution of what was transpiring in the psychoanalytic office.

Every psychoanalytic space bears the imprint of the proprietor of that office, though in general, the physical structure of psychoanalytic office space seems to dictate: look inside, not out; if you see, do not touch. These guidelines have the value of keeping attention on the inner realm, reducing the likelihood of boundary violations and ensuring a sense of general safety. However, as these injunctions have been passed down from psychoanalytic generation to generation, they have become an unquestioned code of behavior. As such, there is often a restrictive atmosphere that perpetuates the requirement of sightlessness, and a wealth of observations remain underutilized.

The attire of both analyst or analysand can sometimes take on therapeutic significance. A number of years ago, I heard an analyst's clinical presentation describing her own early experience in a lengthy analysis (Corpt, 2013). During the almost decade long, multiple-times-per-week treatment, most sessions ended with an important but never discussed visual experience. As the analysand rose from the couch, she would notice the analyst staring at her shoes. She would feel a stab of shame, as she imagined the analyst, a highly trained and sophisticated woman from a family of prominence, judging her own impoverished and uneducated family background based on her choice of apparel. None of this was ever attended to, so this woman never found out whether the analyst in fact harbored a haughty appraisal of her social status or if the analyst simply had an unstated interest in footwear.

The overlooked area of how people dress and adorn themselves is the subject of a paper by Debra Roth, who argues for "a continuous motion of reciprocal influence between exterior and interior aspects of the self" (Roth, 2006, p. 181). Why has the surface been off limits in psychoanalysis? According to Roth:

> What lies at the surface is, in the end, mostly superficial – and what is superficial is both consciously and unconsciously branded as trivial. In other words, psychoanalysis tends to undervalue even complicated surfaces as a result of biases against their visibility, accessibility, and compatibility with some of the more complicated and overdetermined aspects of femininity.
>
> (Roth, 2006, pp. 180–181)

The skin and the organs at its surface "flow continuously from the external surface of the body into its internal cavities" (Roth, 2006, p. 183). Inside and outside are not the solid boundaries that they were once thought to be. Edgar Levenson

(1972) challenged the notion that insight derived from interpretation – a verbal process that entitles the intellect – was the action and goal of psychoanalysis. Forty years later, Rachel Peltz (2012) wrote:

> What we sense comes first, before any knowledge can be derived. Certainly within the discipline of psychoanalysis we are coming to the conclusion again, that knowledge can function as a refuge from experience. And so we must return to the seat of experience on the path to expanding what we can know.
>
> (p. 1)

FROM MIND–BODY DUALITY TO EMBODIMENT

There is a growing recognition in psychoanalysis of the importance of embodiment (Dosamantes-Beaudry, 1997; Knoblauch, 2007; Rappoport, 2012), perhaps, in reaction to the loss of nature through the impact of rapid technological change. Paul Lippmann (2011) suggests that people are slowly becoming machines: "They are in our hand, at our ear, implanted in our bodies, involved in our sexual pleasures, at birth, at death, in our nurseries, in our emotions, in our dreams" (p. 4). I also think that the interest in the body and its sensations reflects an increased willingness on the part of psychoanalysts to acknowledge unknowingness. The de-centering of authority in psychoanalysis from the single, and superior mind of the analyst, to the relationship between the two parties in the room, has also shifted attention from knowledge to experience and from head to body.

How then do analysts remain human and honor the complex nature of the psychoanalytic endeavor brought into their offices daily? A patient recently used the term "the thing in itself" as he was struggling to express his painstaking journey to identify what it is he wants and which is so frustratingly elusive. The phrase originates in a distinction posited by the German philosopher Immanuel Kant, who said a thing exists independent of human observation. What the thing is, in and of itself, independent of any perceiver's view of it, isn't fully knowable in Kant's view (Johnson, 2014). While the patient was using Kant's term somewhat imperfectly, he seemed to be pointing to a place in himself, and with me in the psychoanalytic office, that he was in the process of seeing. When one truly sees something (whether in one's self, in the other, or in the spaces in between), one is honoring the unique perspective of each party and expanding vision itself for both patient and psychoanalyst.

THE IMAGE AND DREAMING

Gaston Bachelard's (1958/1994) observations about the rich significance of early homes and their images could be said about psychoanalytic offices: they shelter daydreaming, protect the dreamer, and allow one to dream in peace. Dreaming is the metaphor, and often the process, by which images become transformed.

For example, I had this dream when I was thinking about how imagery informs therapy:

> I am in a house with a woman. I go to the door to see who is there only to find I am standing in a new space. In this position, I can see the woman down one corridor and realize that a man has entered, and I can see him down another hallway. The architecture of the house allows me to see both, but neither can see the other. I am at the vertex of the angle. They are estranged. Now I realize it is a time for them to be reunited. There is some confusion about my relationship to each one of these figures. But then I experience a comfort, as I apprehend that each is part of me and I am each of them. It is a vision that I am having.

The dream expresses my occupation with photography and writing about images, spatial dimensions, vision, and psychoanalysis. The dream helps me to see by showing me what I am looking at. It seems to be cautioning me about tunnel vision and encouraging me to move from side to side and back again into the eyes of the beholder.

I apply meaning to the image in the dream through association. I think of the Leica M camera, which I have always wanted but felt was beyond my means. Financially? Artistically? It was the camera of choice for the photojournalists and street photographers that first inspired my involvement in photography, like Alfred Eisenstaedt, Henri Cartier-Bresson, Diane Arbus, and Gary Winogrand. It's a rangefinder camera, showing two images when you look through the viewfinder. The photographer then rotates the lens until the two images converge and become one, in focus. The two people in the dream are estranged. Do they represent different versions of myself I am trying to bring together? The writer of intellectual complexity and the poet of evocative language?

My dream appears hopeful. The woman and the man are likely representations of the feminine and masculine in me. Is the comfort I experience in bringing them together in myself an illusion to annihilate fear of separation (McDougall, 1992) or a growing development in myself of seeing gender as more softly assembled (A. Harris, 2000) and more available for psychological flexibility? The image of the two figures is a study in vision. How does an image exist? And what is the relationship between image and language? As soon as language – the kind associated with thinking and verbal expression – comes to the forefront, its immediate relatives, narrative and meaning, are not far behind. There is some indication that people can think before they learn to speak (Hespos & Spelke, 2004). This suggests that an important means of self-expression precedes verbal language. When one's mind "sees" an image, one may be having a primary experience prior to thinking, perhaps even before the "unthought known" (Bollas, 1987). It is the sensorium's unconscious that is engaged and being formed when the image emerges.

The French philosopher Maurice Merleau-Ponty, who explored seeing and language (Lefort, 1968), has recently been discovered by psychoanalysts (Civitarese, 2014; Peltz, 2014), who link sight and language with the intermediary position of thirdness, in contrast to the view of a subordinate body ordered by a transcendent mind. In his work, Merleau-Ponty (1968) provides an example of the phenomenon of touching one hand with the other, illustrating two dimensions of what he terms one's "flesh" (p. 133). That is, people's bodies (each hand in his example) touch and are touched. There is an intertwining of what is object and what is subject. In extending his concept of touch to sight, he says:

> There is a circle of the touched and the touching, the touch takes hold of the touching; there is a circle of the visible and the seeing, the seeing is not without visible existence; there is even an inscription of the touching in the visible, of the seeing in the tangible.
>
> (Merleau-Ponty, 1968, p. 143)

The hand that touches something is, itself, subject to being touched (Toadvine, 2018). And by extension, an eye that sees is subject to being seen. I believe this has some powerful clinical implications. For example, self-disclosure may be conceived of as the desire and freedom to see, before language joins into the experience. One may ask, what is being revealed by looking? When people look, they are showing their interest. What is at risk? Exposure to what interests one? Do analysts shy away from seeing because they intuit it will result in their becoming more visible to their patients? A patient told me of an experience of sitting in a cafe at a table, off to the side, and having a full view of good-looking, lightly dressed people walking by on the first warm day of the year. Awareness of pleasure was mixed with the inhibiting feeling of not wanting to be seen looking. His experience of hiding his desire to see reminded me of when I worked in a clinic early in my career. Each clinician had to do a number of weekly initial evaluations and report to the group. Often the woman or man being interviewed was said to be "attractive," but no one ever admitted, "I was attracted to this person." To say so would have resulted in being seen or in being caught in looking.

A clinical example may illustrate the complexities inherent in seeing and being seen in analysis. Here is a dream from a female patient:

> I'm in a store with a former boyfriend. I see a toy – seems like a vintage toy – and pick it up. It has different parts and buttons that, when you press or manipulate them somehow, make other things happen. Can't quite recall what, but it's very cool. I am eager to show it to him and he is really fascinated.

I am fascinated with this short dream. The patient has been dreaming more lately, or at least, she has been reporting more dreams recently. She worried when she came in to treatment that she might not be interesting enough, even to herself. She did not feel recognized as a child by her parents. The patient is an artist who struggled mightily to overcome harsh parental criticism for creative risks she took while growing up. She recalls being punished and feeling humiliated for her efforts, which she now sees as early artistic strivings. In one instance, when she was a small girl, she cobbled together a costume and made a float for a small parade in her town. She did not get any guidance from her parents in constructing her entry. When she saw what the other children had made, she felt a deep shame for the results of her creativity. She felt she was simply not creative, a self-assessment reinforced by her mother's frequent critiques.

Now as she shows me this dream in therapy, I try to see the toy and its source of fascination. Could the toy represent her, prior to therapy, and the former boy-friend represent me? Is the dream telling how, through our work together, she can reclaim her playfulness and creativity? That she finds places in herself that "can make things happen"? Is the toy a gadget, like a remote-control device? Or does it have a robotic-human quality to it? What are the other things that happen when the buttons are pressed or the parts manipulated? Can I meet her eagerness with wanting to show this cool toy with my own fascination in seeing? Is there some-thing sexual in this dream, or is the erotic implication only in my mind's eye? Will raising these questions be awkward for her? It feels awkward for me. I feel shy. Are we recreating opportunities for liberation of creative urges, or are we about to be plunged into shame? Kilborne (2002), writing about disappearance, referenced Jean Paul Sartre's definition of shame. The essence of what constitutes shame is not the committing of a particular fault, not being a guilty object, "but in general of being an object, that is, of recognizing myself in this degraded, fixed and depend-ent being" (1964, p. 264). Shame results from the self-consciousness of needing the other, of a deep dependency on relationship.

Early in our work together, we discussed art and the history of the male art-ist's gaze and the subjugation of the female model. Once, in a session when the patient was exhausted, she lay on the couch and almost fell asleep. There was a long silent period, and I began to doodle on a writing pad nearby. Soon after I began to sketch the scene in front of me. This time, as the image was taking shape, I felt a certain uneasiness. I told her about the experience and asked if she wanted to see it. She did, and not much was made of it at the time, but I had felt very engaged as I sketched her on the couch, thinking it was a good artistic rendering. But after I showed it to her, and when there was little response, I felt I had done something wrong and devalued my own creative effort. This incident preceded her dream, so I now have all these associations and questions. What would be most helpful for this patient? By seeing, I inevitably open the door to being seen. She has bravely shown me her dream, and it feels important to meet her gaze with mine. What will it mean to make things happen?

TWO TYPES OF IMAGES

How can images aid analysts as they seek meaning with their patients, with the patient's dream images, and with the analyst's own images in dreams and else-where? Images occur both in the surround and in the mind – that is, they are both exterior and interior. An image can be a material representation, as in a pho-tograph. An image also refers to a mental picture, as in an imagined impression.

What links both forms of image is visual experience. One must see to visualize the thing in one's mind. Once something is seen, it can be transformed, as it becomes available as an internalized object. A particularly important variant of this process is when the act of seeing gets infused with emotion and creates an imagined, evocative image.

As I reflect on this process, with photography and psychoanalysis easily standing in for one another, the following thoughts seem to apply to images in both endeavors: now you see it; now you don't. You catch a glimpse of something in your eye. Appearance and disappearance. An image exists somewhere, and the eye has transferred the experience to the mind. In the dark room of the photographic studio or the psychoanalytic office, there is often little or no illumination. Yet once an image has caught the eye, there is the possibility of a wish to see. What happens in the juncture between first sight and what follows? Will there be distraction, excitement, insight, or groping in darkness? There must be exposure to the receptive and vulnerable material, the photographic paper and the psychoanalytic eye, that holds the potential for the image to emerge. And if it is revealed, content and meaning may emerge. Will the image survive? And for what purpose?

THE PHOTOGRAPHIC IMAGE

The photo-messaging application Snapchat allows for images to be communicated and then self-destruct in under ten seconds. This phenomenon is in stark contrast to the sense of a photograph as a symbol of visible permanence. M. Gerard Fromm, describing one of the important functions that photography played in a young man's life following the death of his mother, said, "Time seems capable of being halted. . . . A photograph . . . offer(s) a poignant experience of being with, a union sheltered from interruption and unconcerned with aging" (1989, p. 300).

Roland Barthes, the French philosopher mentioned in Chapter 4 who wrote a classic investigation of photography, *Camera Lucida* (1981), took time to find the right image of his recently dead mother. It was not simply a picture of her that he sought but one that captured an essence of who she was (to him). Looking over numerous photographs from different periods of her life, he was waiting to discover one in which he would recognize her. Finally, he found it the Winter Garden photograph:

> I studied the little girl and at last rediscovered my mother. The distinctiveness of her face, the naive attitude of her hands, the place she had docilely taken without either showing or hiding herself, and finally her expression, which distinguished her. . . . In this little girl's image, I saw the kindness that had formed her being immediately and forever.
>
> (Barthes, 1981, p. 69)

Barthes was looking for this image among her belongings in the apartment in which she had died. The objects there were nostalgically associated with his mother and the memories (really the sense) of the many times he had been in that place with her. As in any space, especially one that has been occupied for a long time, there was probably a distinctive atmosphere to the rooms. Sight, sound, smell, and other sensory processes defined the feel of the place. These impressions held the presence and absence of Barthes's mother and his relationship with her. The photograph for him was "both my mother's being and my grief at her death" (Barthes, 1981, p. 70). This experience was deeply personal. Although he was able, perhaps needed, to write about the experience, he did not include the photograph in his small book filled with numerous other photographs. He explained parenthetically:

> I cannot reproduce the Winter Garden photograph. It exists only for me. For you, it would be nothing but an indifferent picture, one of the thousand manifestations of "ordinary" . . . at most it would interest. . . [you from the perspective of the] period, clothes, photogeny; but in it for you, no wound.
>
> (Barthes, 1981, p. 73)

Photography and psychoanalysis are both places to seek encounters with evocative images and to experience the joy of discovering what was lost or may never have existed. Photography and psychoanalysis also share commonalities in connecting one to the grief of finding the wound, identifying losses, and getting a glimpse of the dread of death. I took a photograph in 1971 in Encino, California. It is a grainy, black-and-white picture that is out of focus. Hard to distinguish in the picture is a chair, a white shirt hanging from a bookcase piled with papers, folders, and books. There is a big window, and outside it appears to be nighttime, or maybe it's the reflection of the room's lighting. When I look at the picture, I vaguely remember there had been a recent large earthquake, and I can almost sense the presence of an aftershock. It is not a particularly dramatic image, but it is very evocative for me, since it pictures my analyst's office from that time period. I think that I took the photo when he had stepped out of the room.

This image is accompanied by memories of the time I spent in that office with my analyst, Irwin Bloom, during the time period when I had returned to school and begun my graduate study in preparation for becoming an analyst myself. During those years, I often felt lost and disconnected from my career dream. I struggled with the research design in constructing my doctoral dissertation and spent many hours in small, windowless cubicles of hospitals and outpatient clinics that were the sites of my work. I feel nurtured, however, through that remembered image, connecting with my recalled desires, wishes, and hopes. In becoming an analyst, I found the solution to my career and life dilemma and at the same time always could remain in that special space that is psychoanalysis – by practicing psychoanalysis. Although for a long time I dared not tell anyone of this special motive, I longed for my own office in which to practice and live this work. Nowadays, however, we accept that the practice of psychoanalysis not only can transform the patient but also the therapist (Atwood, 2015). All this personal history and psychological development are connected to a single image.

THE PATIENT AND THE OFFICE

An experience I had as a patient may serve to illustrate how the office, patient, analyst, and image and the past, present, and future are intertwined with seeing and not being able to see (Gerald, 2011). In this instance, there were only a few minutes left in the session, which ended with a period of silence. Quite unexpectedly, I said, "I wish you could stay a little longer." I didn't know I would say this until the words were out of my mouth. As soon as the sentence was uttered, a rush of feeling came over me. I tried to speak, but my voice broke into a sob. I was surrounded by the familiar comfort of the analytic room, but I also knew I was alone. Nonetheless, the quiet presence of my analyst was palpable. I could make out his rhythmic breathing. Our years of working together was a constant I had come to rely on.

The next image that came to my mind was of my father, long deceased. I could see him clearly. My utterance, wishing for more time, took on a deep longing for all that had been missed. My father had seen me only as a boy, never knew me as I grew to be a man, marry, have children, or grow in my career. I cried deeply yet felt enlivened as the session ended. I would have wanted to hug my analyst, but this was not possible. The session was being conducted by telephone. I looked around the room. It was my office. My analyst was in his own office, 150 miles away. With a couple of exceptions over the course of our working together, when I had visited him in his place, all our sessions had been over the phone. I was alone but in the presence of an image of my dear father. The image had arrived in the context of a great many factors. The material in the session that was being discussed was part of an associative network. The statement of longing, itself seeming to arrive as a momentary impulse, was the obvious correlate of the emergence of the image of my dead father. The larger themes that were part of the transference relationship in the therapy were most likely important contributors to what occurred in my mind's eye. Finally, my visual orientation, honed in photography and drawing, predisposed me to imagery.

Telephone sessions have become an increasing part of contemporary psychoanalytic practice (Leffert, 2003; Lipton, 2001; Scharff, 2012). It is generally understood that there are similarities and differences between telephone therapy and in-person therapy. Distance is breached with the consequence of the possibility of a different kind of intimate connection on the one hand and an added emphasis of separation and loss on the other. Any and all these factors could be explored further to possibly aid in understanding what took place with me. But I am most interested in the contributions of visual imagery that – in subtle, complex, and often unconscious ways – influenced this analytic moment and more generally is a factor in the experience with patients in our psychoanalytic spaces. The visual field in psychoanalysis encompasses the physical existence and appearance of the patient and the analyst, the spaces in which analysis takes place, and the wealth of imagery that each party brings with them into the analytic relationship. What surrounds and faces analysts are essential components for finding and generating evocative imagery for psychoanalytic work. Much of this wealth lies in the recesses of our visual–emotional vaults.

In my office, there were many places for me to look at while I was on the phone in the session previously described. For example, in my sight line is a series of postcards placed around a mirror that sits atop an armoire. A patient who is a photographer once commented, "Those postcards must all be parts of you." This seemingly simple observation hit home in a powerful way; I somehow had never seen the truth of what I was presenting. And somewhere in the hard drive of my visual repertoire is the picture of my analyst's office from the few times I visited him there. There was a plethora of visual objects in his room, some of which joined with my collection of postcards. I think we might share an image of Franz Kafka. My space expanded to include his office and the images in it, so there was an opening to more than what I was looking at. I could see for 150 miles. When I first visited his office, I felt we were somehow related in aesthetic sensibility . . . and maybe more. His office was completely different from mine yet seemed deeply and emotionally familiar.

As I have already mentioned, I first became intrigued with the offices people work in when as a child I accompanied my father to work during school vacations. I found a place to play inside his professional office with its large wooden desk, swivel chairs, file cabinets, adding machine, typewriter, ledger sheets in heavy bound books, pencils, pens, and ink jars. The space and its objects had meaning because of whose room it was and the nature of our relationship: he was my father, and I was his son. This basic truth of how people's relationships are intertwined with rooms and their contents certainly applies to psychoanalytic spaces. Analysts and their patients inhabit the spaces, and these spaces live in the analysts and analysands. Each brings the history of previously occupied spaces and spent time in each of their respective interior homes.

So, as I sat in my office, as a patient, talking with my analyst on the phone, I was in a multi-determined space. I was surrounded by my professional home, with its evocative objects. But there also was a visible presence of what was invisible. I could not transport my body through space or back in time to these other territories. Yet my eyes had registered their existence, and they were now permanently part of my visual being. They were felt images. My analyst's office, my father's office, and my childhood home were all within sight, and I longed to have more time to spend with them.

7 The relational image

Creating a psychoanalytic photographic portrait

I was once invited to participate on a panel discussing the creative process, and in thinking about what I might say, I remembered the words of French photographer Frederic Brenner. When asked why he had embarked upon a project of photographing people of the Jewish Diaspora, creating portraits of people in more than 40 countries over a 25-year period, Brenner said, "We do what we do, not because of what we know, but because of what we don't know" (2003). A hopeful consequence of being engaged in a long-term project with another (such as in the psychoanalytic relationship) is that we learn more about ourselves and the other and about engaged relationships themselves, and this process produces surprises and a continuing appreciation of being all too human. Along the way, we might catch a glimpse of why the endeavor was so compelling to begin with.

My own long-term project of photographing psychoanalysts in their offices has provided me with an opportunity to reflect on my professional identity and creative process, and I have reaped some of the benefits already mentioned. It is no small thing to hold a camera, either as an amateur or professional. The great photojournalist Alfred Eisenstaedt was known for some of the most famous portraits of the twentieth century: Albert Einstein, Marlene Dietrich, Winston Churchill, Sophia Loren, and an amazing series of photographs of Joseph Goebbels, Hitler's minister of propaganda. When the Jewish German-born American photographer was asked how it felt to shoot Goebbels, he replied, "When I have a camera in my hand I don't know fear." The resulting image, which apparently caught Goebbels off guard since he was smiling before being approached by Eisenstaedt, shows the despotic quality of this Nazi and has been known as the "Eyes of Hate" photograph (Cosgrove, 2014).

Edmund Engelman (1976, p. 131), the Jewish-Austrian photographer of Freud's office, approached his photography assignment in Nazi-occupied Vienna with trepidation:

> I was both excited and afraid as I walked through the empty streets toward Bergasse 19 that wet May morning in 1938. . . . I was convinced that anyone who saw me would instantly know that I was on my way to the offices of Dr. Sigmund Freud – on a mission that would hardly have pleased the Nazis.

Irene Engelman, CSW
West End Avenue
New York, New York
May 17, 2004

My project exists in the shadow of both Freud and Engelman – dwarfed by Engelman's courage but certainly inspired by it. I was fortunate enough to meet, interview, and photograph Engelman's widow, Irene Engelman, a psychoanalytic therapist in New York, and hear about the harrowing and intrigue-filled events that were part of the creation of those relational images of Freud and his space.

Each photoshoot (similar to a psychoanalytic session) contains the circumstances and dynamics of the subject, the setting, and the relationship between photographer and subject. There is always some uncertainty in anticipating the shoot. What will it be like for me and for my subject, and will the resulting image do justice to our experience? In my early correspondence with analysts I intend to photograph, I may ask them to describe the space they work in and something about their sense of inhabiting that space. Some might include images of the office along with a description. One analyst, after writing about the decor and design of her office, concluded by saying:

> It's funny, as I'm writing this I see how these things are the essence of me . . . places I have gone with people I love, gifts from dear friends and family, comfortability and finger puppets to ease the seriousness of the work we do.
>
> (personal communication, Luly Casares, February 26, 2011)

After each portrait session, I spend time looking over the images: digitals on computer screen and hard copy of the film on contact sheets. This part of the process is undertaken to select the one picture that is most representative of my experience of this person. I am looking for an elusive message in the image that says: "Here I am in this space, and you are seeing me despite the obstacles that each of us brings to this complicated and contradictory experience of wanting to be recognized and protecting against such an intimate and vulnerable moment." In this chapter, I unpack the process of creating one of these *relational images* in the series and also show how the relational image is also in a relationship with death.

PHOTOGRAPHY AS A HEALING ART

I discovered photography in 1963, the year my father died. I had been in his bedroom when a doctor attempted to revive him from a fatal heart attack, but I became dissociated from the experience. Five months later, President Kennedy was killed. Anyone old enough to have retained the memory of that day remembered it for the rest of their lives. People recall exactly where they were on that fateful November day. I was 18 and a freshman in college, but I have no memory of that historic event. These two memory lapses became conflated, when I dissociated from my immediate grief caused by those traumas. I took up photography following these traumatic losses. Only years later, when I happened to read an article in a psychoanalytic text, did I realize the connection between loss and photography. Photography was an attempt to regulate the increasing sense of

Luly Casares, Ph.D.
Ponce de Leon Boulevard Coral
Gables, Florida
February 28, 2011

panic associated with my experience of mortality: looking at the world through the protective lens of a camera produced new and less annihilating images. In "Photography as Transitional Functioning," Fromm (1989) provided a clinical example of how a patient used photography not just to defend against painful and dangerous inner states but also to serve a transitional function of opening up potential space to express creativity (Winnicott, 1953). This was also true for me.

The office is a contextual source of powerful resonances for sanctuary from and entry into disturbance (Gerald, 2011, 2013, 2015). It is in rooms such as the psychoanalytic office that we have the condition of privacy to explore our darkest nightmares. In such rooms we also return to face again the loss of early trust with the modest hope of regaining it with another.

The bedroom of my father's death, with its associations to my parents' intimate life, to his work office where he conducted his independent practice of accounting, and the psychoanalytic offices I have occupied as patient, supervisee, student, and analyst have coalesced into a transitional space. These places are part mine and part other, where seeing and being seen are both prohibited and encouraged. They are welcoming sanctuaries for mutual vulnerability as well as dreaded enclosures echoing with the terror of exclusion and exile. Photography itself, and particularly the camera used in a photographic portrait, can likewise become a "room" for potential space. This instrument can separate and bring together subject and photographer in the effort see each other. It is no wonder, in retrospect, that I came upon the project of applying my photographic eye, in its protective and creative functions, to the spaces that represent both a trailing edge of loss and a prospective position for a creative future (Aron & Atlas, 2015).

Photographing the psychoanalytic office always involves a sense of loss, due to its ongoing link with the first iconic office in Vienna, swept away by Nazism, and the uncertainty about whether psychoanalysis would continue, even though it has continued and maintained its vibrancy through theoretical adaptations (Gerald, 2011). Photographing these spaces, alive with the analysts in them, allows for the illusion of preserving them forever. Yet we are all somehow connected to the "death" of that first office and its closure under pressure from the Nazis. The end of Freud's office became associated with his escape to England, where the master would die little more than a year later. The inevitable termination of every psychoanalytic office and of the people who inhabit them hovers over the lively images of the psychoanalysts I photograph and shades all our work. The start of every psychoanalytic encounter also contains the seeds of its ending. Doctoral clinical psychology students seeing patients in their first-year internships learn from the start they must begin to plan for the termination of therapy. In more extended analytic work, there is ample room for the illusion that the relationship is timeless. But despite the accoutrements of the psychoanalytic office and the invitation for a freely associative sanctuary removed from the ticking clock of life, "the end is contained in the beginning . . . like a foretaste of death" (George Orwell, 1950/1977, p. 159).

THE RELATIONAL IMAGE

My concept of the relational image has been honed by working at the intersection of photography and psychoanalysis. The relational image is the result of the action of mutual vulnerability, whereby being seen while in the act of anxiously looking (where there is a great deal at stake), creates a new image that allows for both the contradiction and interdependence of darkness, disturbance, despair, and death on the one hand and light, connection, love, and living on the other. To be sure, not all photographic images are relational, in the sense that I am using this term; many images objectify and distance subject and object (Morris, 2011; Sontag, 1973), denying the vulnerability of the all-seeing photographer/agent.

I consider the experience of seeing and being seen in psychoanalysis to be a central struggle in the psychoanalytic endeavor. Because psychoanalysis privileges hearing over seeing (Fuss & Sanders, 2004; Levenson, 2003), we analysts have been visually impaired as we have lived in the shadow of Freud's couch. As Levenson (2003) has said, "The entire psychoanalytic praxis, although annotated in words, actually takes place in a visual-spatial modality" (p. 233). He proposed that transference and countertransference are created in psychoanalysis through the analyst imagining (visualizing) the patient's narrative. I add that the process of visualizing and creating images that both precede and stem from what is said occurs for both the patient and the analyst, and actually seeing one another is at the heart of this process. Therapeutic action can be thought of as the creation of new relational images that allow for disturbance and distress to be transformed into more tolerable visions.

In the clinical situation, a perceptual-cognitive model is the basis for how therapist and patient take in the other. I believe that this occurs in the very earliest phase of encounter, from the sounds of the voice on the phone to the first impression of the initial consultation, so that patient and analyst have a structure in which to see and try to understand the other. This process is largely unconscious and based on each person's personal history. While the process can facilitate a recognition of the other as "something/someone I have encountered before, maybe not unlike me," it also is a restricted portrait of another complex human being. Over the course of acting on the other, in the shared analytic transference, especially upon areas of vulnerability, the possibility emerges of reconfiguring our experience of who we are with, and of seeing the other and ourselves with fresh eyes. From this perspective, new images may be revealed, mutually created at the most fragile junctures. Seeing, as both a sensory activity and as a precondition for recognition (Beebe, Rustin, Sorter, & Knoblauch, 2003; Benjamin, 1990), is made clearer and goes deeper when it is linked with the experience of death and loss and the capacity to survive and create.

PHOTOGRAPHING ANASTASIOS

Anastasios Gaitanidis is a psychoanalyst of Greek extraction living in London, England. This photographic portrait will be used to describe the process of creating a relational image and the related developing relationship between photographer and subject prior to and following the actual photoshoot. Each of the photographs in the project, as well as the project as a whole, illustrate the central features of what I am describing as a relational image. I use the experience of this "psycho-analytic" photoshoot and the creation of a photographic image as a metaphor for the creation of relational images in the psychoanalytic experience.

I first heard about Anastasios through an email from an esteemed colleague, who asked if I would meet with him when he came to town to attend the American Psychological Association's annual division conference on psychoanalysis. Dr. Gaitanidis was considering relocating to New York. Attached to my colleague's email was a letter from Dr. Gaitanidis and a curriculum vitae introducing himself. We met for lunch and seemed to immediately connect. I was struck by the soulfulness of this Greek man, who left his homeland to attend college in England and remained there. I was drawn to and connected with his dignified face, handsome and revealing of both joy and sorrow. This attraction was amplified when we shared more about our lives, entering into surprising depth at a first meeting. In retrospect, the specter of suffering and death and the commitment to a related and creative life was present from the initial introduction to Anastasios, extended to the lunch in New York, spending time together at presentations at the conference, engaging in the photoshoot itself, keeping in touch by email, and later lunching with my wife and him in South London. Anastasios and I both had been dealing over the past ten years with health concerns, our own and those of loved ones. Not far beneath the surface, we were in touch with anxieties about death and had been in various stages of mourning for a long time.

A few years prior to meeting Anastasios, I had a malignant tumor removed from my spine through two neurological-surgical procedures that involved the re-sectioning of my lumbar vertebrae. In addition to the standard difficulties inherent in major surgery and the pain of a long recovery, I was brought back emotionally to two earlier experiences with death while I was an adolescent and teenager. I began to visualize the physical surroundings and activities that took place in the room in which I watched my father die. I was reversing the message in the dream that Freud had the night after his father's funeral, where he reads a message on the board of the railway station: "It is requested to close the eyes" (Levenson, 1983, p. 17). Did Freud, unable to bear what he called "the greatest loss a man could have," the death of his father, need to become blind to suffering? In contrast, my eyes were beginning to open. I remembered an even earlier brush with death at age 13. Through a medical misdiagnosis, I sustained a life-threatening ruptured appendix. Images from that time, both the disturbance and its recovery, came back into my mind.

Anastasios was bringing his own storage of trauma to our first meeting. He had been living for many years under the cloud of his wife's mortality, following a diagnosis of her cancer early in their marriage. Initial treatment had resulted in a period of remission followed more recently by the return of the disease and a very uncertain prognosis for recovery. In response to an email I sent him, in which I mentioned how busy I had been with not enough time for reflection, Anastasios responded (personal communication, June 20, 2015):

> I agree with you: we need at least two lifetimes. . . . I often find myself automatically responding to life's demands instead of having the necessary time and space to think and feel my way through life's difficulties. I want to prioritize the things that are important to me – like caring for my wife (her condition is stable but still dangerous).

As our relationship developed, it was imbued with excitement, creative expression, the challenge of learning, and the promise of intimacy, as well as with the fear of loss, the anxiousness of uncertainty, and the terror of death. In a series of emails between Anastasios and me, we became acquainted with each other's work, health, spouses, and inner lives. Here are some excerpts:

> Hello Mark,
> . . . I would love to read your paper and see your latest photos as well as see you when you arrive in London. . . . I will also show you my office and you can photograph me in it. . . . I am looking forward to seeing you again.
>
> (June 15, 2014)

> Hi Mark,
> . . . I read and loved your paper. More specifically, I love the fact that you establish strong links between physical space, architecture, and psychoanalysis. I also admired your honest and heartfelt account of the impact of the stain on your rug on both you and your patients (Gerald, 2014). . . . I "daydreamed" . . . a connection to Heidegger's notion of "dwelling" . . . and his privileging architecture as a form of life. I hope we'll have some time to discuss this and other topics during your visit. I cannot wait to see you.
>
> (July 17, 2014)

I had not imagined Anastasios's office beforehand when I met him in London for the photoshoot, nor had we discussed it in our previous meetings or correspondence. I learned that he rented the space from another therapist, and thus the decor and furnishings mostly did not belong to him. The space, in a Victorian house in South London, was warm with a casual yet anomalous Southwest American style. In retrospect, there was a sense of displacement between the person and the room, and this seemed in keeping with the quality of his Greek (and part Jewish) background somewhat displaced in this English setting. Because of the less intimate connection between analyst and room, perhaps I focused more closely on his face and posture and less on the background. And there are times when the body and countenance of a subject seems to encompass the room around them.

Anastasios Gaitanidis, Ph.D.
Lowther Hill
London, England
July 20, 2014

Upon my return to New York, I wrote:

> Dear Anastasios,
>
> I am not sure if I ever wrote to you after my visit to London in July. You were much on my mind, I am afraid I composed the letters in my head and never put them in an email. Please forgive me for being so delayed in thanking you for your gracious hospitality on photographing you and being your guest for lunch. Laini also so enjoyed your company. I have spent time with the images from your photoshoot and really like a number of them. I finally chose my favorite and will send you a print. Hope that you are well. Laini and I have included you and Maria when we toast a glass of wine together, cheers and l'chaim to you both.
>
> (September 7, 2014)

I received this message in reply:

> Dear Mark,
>
> I was very moved by your and Laini's empathic understanding of what I and Maria are currently going through. Of course, you had your own encounter with illness which provides you with an intimate understanding of our situation. Yet, it is not always easy to "genuinely" hear the other's experience and struggle. When you quoted Dylan Thomas's "Don't go gentle into that good night," you really encapsulated how I and Maria feel about our daily "fight," "rage, rage against the dying of the light." I really enjoyed the photoshoot and I'm looking forward to receiving the print of the image you've selected. My warmest regards and love to you and Laini.
>
> (September 14, 2014)

We corresponded in the interim and then I became unsure about whether I had sent a print. I wrote:

> Dear Anastasios,
>
> Did you ever receive the print of the image that I sent? I was just going over my photographs and realized there were two competing images. I'm not sure which one you got.

Anastasios responded immediately:

> Dear Mark,
>
> Maria's condition has deteriorated over the last few months . . . I am planning to take a year's unpaid leave from my university job after Easter so as to be able to spend more time with Maria (she might not be able to survive beyond this summer).
>
> (February 1, 2015)

I realized that I had not sent either image. I was conflicted about the choice. One was a flattering picture of him smiling in the expanse of his borrowed office. I decided upon the other, a much more somber close-up and mailed it to him.

He responded a few days later:

> My dear friend,
> Thank you so much for the print of the photo which I received today. Photographs (like dreams) have the unique quality of arresting time and capturing in an instant what one can barely notice in years. I look as if all the troubles of the world have landed on my shoulders – but my melancholic face is not bitter; it appears to be calm and dignified. This fills me up with hope and the desire to persevere – thank you.
> (February 18, 2015)

A few months later, when I was invited to participate in the panel I mention at the start of this chapter, I wrote to Anastasios for permission to speak about the experience of photographing him and to use our email correspondence. He wrote:

> My dear friend,
> Of course, you have my permission. I would have loved to be there with you and share my experience of the process. However, as I cannot be there, I want to say that for me the photoshoot was embedded within the context of our developing friendship and closeness. After a while, I did not feel that a "you" existed independently over there who photographed "me" over here. Instead, I felt that our connection to each other was present during the process. When I look at the photos, it is not only me that I see – I see you as well, or more precisely, I see the tie that binds us to each other. I see myself as constituted through my relation to you and vice versa. This relational dimension is captured in the photos (this is the power of art in general) but I'm not sure how any narrative can do justice to this dimension. Any attempt to tell "the" story about the relational dimension of these photos will necessarily falter. But that does not mean that we should be reduced to speechlessness, that we should not tell "a" story about what is (and must remain) fundamentally ineffable. "I must go on, I cannot go on, I will go on." Thank you again for sending me these wonderful photos.
> (March 15, 2015)

Maria died in November after many years of her struggle with cancer. Anastasios' paraphrase from Samuel Beckett's novel (1958) proved to be prophetic. He does go on.

PSYCHOANALYSIS, DEATH, AND PHOTOGRAPHY

Psychoanalysis has had a troubling relationship with death. Freud's theories can be seen as minimizing the reality of death and death anxiety, even though a death instinct is assumed. According to Razinsky (2014) and Yalom (2008), Freud posited that death cannot be understood by the unconscious and, therefore, the fear of death is always a stand-in for some other source of anxiety. These theoretical contradictions are in strong contrast to Freud's own statements about death, indicated in his personal correspondence. He acknowledged to a patient that he thought about the possibility of death every day. He also revealed in a letter to a respected colleague, after learning of the death of the colleague's son, that his theory of mourning could not replace the depth of certain losses. This letter of April 12, 1939, is written on the anniversary of the death of Freud's own daughter, Sophie, five months before his own death:

> Although we know that after such a loss the acute state of mourning will subside, we also know that we shall remain inconsolable and will never find a substitute. No matter what may fill the gap, even if it be filled completely, it nevertheless remains something else.
>
> (Frankiel, 1994, p. 70)

His colleague, reflecting on Freud's letter years later, wrote, "When compared with Freud's discussion in his 'Mourning and Melancholia,' [the letter] . . . suffices by itself to show how far Freud the man surpasses Freud the scientist in largeness and depth of humanity" (Frankiel, 1994, p. 69). In spite of our elaborate and elegant theories, we are conscious beings who must live with the continual knowledge of our own mortality.

The death of a parent when a person is still young creates significant challenges to their sense of security and trust in their continual being. Yet exposure to death at an early age can provide a basis for the struggle to find an outlet of creative expression. Even as my eyes shut in the presence of death, they opened to a deeper poignancy of the fragility and sanctity of living. Whatever it is that guides human attraction, whether complementarity or similarity, I have often been drawn to those with sadness in their eyes. I was told while growing up that I resembled my mother, while my sister looked like my father's side. As a boy, I often felt uncomfortable with this female connection, but as I grew I could see myself in her eyes and she in mine. Her father had died when she was young, so perhaps we shared a vision of mourning. I found this same visual pull in gazing into the eyes of the subject of the photoshoot, Anastasios Gaitanidis.

Losing a significant other at a young age can also create a frozen emotional condition. This hardened state is associated with split off, "not-me" zones that are kept from joining a person's primary identity. As reminders of the earlier trauma come closer to awareness, a feeling of becoming overwhelmed encroaches in the form of an annihilating threat. Defenses are enacted. Creative expression (an urge for life) that touches upon the raw disturbance but is shaped by the artist as a re-imaging of the early event can thaw the impacted trauma. When a young person loses a parent or other person to whom they have a deep connection, it may be necessary for them to become immediately attracted to a replacement for the missing person so they do not become frozen. In studying children and adolescents who had lost a parent, Wolfenstein (1966) concluded mourning, as described by Freud as successfully relinquishing the attachment to the dead loved one, did not occur in her young patients. She proposed that until the successful resolution of adolescence – with its Kleinian achievement of the depressive position, the relinquishment of the childhood fantasy of omnipotence – the child or adolescent does not possess the developmental tools to accept the loss and move on.

Although I find the deterministic quality of such theories objectionable, I was struck by the recognition of my teenage self in Wolfenstein's description of her patients: "We have observed repeatedly that some children and adolescents begin to decline in their school performance following the death of a parent. In . . . other instances, truancy . . . begins after a parent has died" (1966, p. 347). I also identified with the initial feeling of deep shame that these kids experienced. One feels, in losing a parent, personally negligent, as if one has not carefully protected an object of great value. Finding photography and the connections reflected in sad faces of persons and places of the late 1960s relieved some of the shame for me. Protected by a sturdy camera, I found a space to mourn and celebrate the marginality of being a loser, a validation of having experienced loss.

In addition to photographing people on the street, I was especially drawn to portraits. There was something compelling, yet disquieting, in the necessary encounter with another human being. Photography as a medium of self-expression allows for numerous opportunities to move closer and further away from what you are seeing, from what you wish to see. Cameras, lenses, film, lights, all provide ways of dialing into or out of connection with one's subject. The digital delete button is the contemporary means of avoiding an intersection with what is not pleasing. Yet as a photographer, one is always potentially the subject of one's own work, as well as in a mutually open relationship with the one who is being photographed. Even early on, when I was protected from knowing what I was after in this activity, I sensed I was looking into the abyss with the hope that I would see my own reflection, and the death I dreaded would be transformed into a live image.

An early photograph I took in the late 1960s first confirmed for me the enormous power of seeing myself by looking through a photographic lens. I realized years later that the creation of this portrait – of my wife Laini listening to music – was the beginning of my own desire to create photographic portraits. While walking around our apartment with my camera, I saw her sitting in reverie, listening to a recording of Joan Baez. The immaculate, clear, and piercing voice blended with the young woman cradling herself, her hands and feet creating an intricate web that rooted her to the bench and in the sad beauty that the moment evoked. Although the photographer, I was part of the space captured in my lens, my own forlorn self – restless yet strangely quiet like my subject, longing to be freed from the unpredictable waves of anxiety that held me in their grip.

The privileged view of psychoanalysts and photographers allows them to slow down time. Their common mantra could be "stop and look": outside and inside;

Laini Gerald Grand
Central Parkway
Queens, New York
Circa late 1960s

past, present, and future; between you and me; light and dark; death and hope, all in the service of creating a new relational image. In one of the few papers on photography in the psychoanalytic literature, Donald Colson (1979) links photography to time, change, and mourning. He recalls how a colleague expressed how, when photographing his children, he was struck with a poignant sense of the rapid passage of time.

The presence of death can be overwhelming, particularly when death arrives precipitously. Colson addresses photography's appeal at times of bewildering shifts. "People take up photography at times of rapid change in their lives when the photograph is most clearly expressive of the wish to hold time still, to have greater opportunity to consolidate the ordinarily fleeting experience of the moment" (Colson, 1979, p. 274). Fromm also notes photography's capacity to stop time: "A photograph seems to offer a poignant experience of being with, a union sheltered from interruption and unconcerned with aging" (Fromm, 1989, p. 30). And Cole says, "Photography is inescapably a memorial art. It selects, out of the flow of time, a moment to be preserved, with the moments before and after falling away like sheer cliffs" (Cole, 2015, p. 24).

James Hamilton's (1995) study of the life and work of eminent American photographer Edward Weston shows how a photographer used his camera to both mourn and memorialize his mother. Hamilton's thesis is that Weston's photography is an adaptive response to the trauma of his mother's death from pneumonia when Weston was five. Hamilton found in Weston's photographs, journal entries, letters, and transcripts of interviews with the photographer evidence of the "piercing" effects of early loss on his being and artistry. Referring to the loss of his mother, Weston says, "all that returns to me of her – are a pair of black piercing eyes – burning eyes – maybe burning with fever" (Hamilton, 1995, p. 681). Hamilton's beautiful photographs of landscapes, still lifes, nudes, and portraits are efforts to restore the lost love of his mother by capturing or visually incorporating an aesthetically pleasing image. Speaking about one of his cameras (and perhaps of how it served as a bridge to recreate his mother), Weston said, "I needed no friends now. I was always alone with my love" (Hamilton, 1995, p. 680). This statement about his cameras resonated with me, since I felt the same way about my own early cameras. Their solid "polished steel," seemingly capable of securing "pulsating flesh," provided a passage from death to life. This sense of a secure passage between the darkness and light is what I equate, in a rough analogy, with the partnership between analyst and patient and photographer and subject. They are held safely in the mutual vulnerability of intimacy, one for the other.

MOURNING AND CREATIVE LIFE

In describing what he calls "the art of mourning," Thomas Ogden (2000) emphasizes that to mourn involves making something "adequate to the experience of loss." This art, whether done by a formal artist or an ordinary person, "represent(s) the individual's effort to meet, to be equal to, to do justice to, the fullness and complexity of his or her relationship to what has been lost and to the experience of loss itself" (p. 66). Each one mourns using their particular and distinctive gifts of self-expression: "As one would expect, a musician will mourn by "making music," a painter will mourn in the act of painting, an analyst in the experience of engaging in an analytic relationship or perhaps in the experience of writing about (and from) his or her analytic experiences" (Ogden, 2000, p. 66). The particularity of one's being is central to the process of mourning and the quality of artistic transformation.

Imminent death and mourning – for what was lost and what will be lost in the future – are driving forces behind people's need to express themselves, especially in aesthetic creations. This is not a new idea. Ernest Becker (1973) argued persuasively that the majority of human activity is undertaken primarily to deny death. Christopher Bollas (1989), influenced by Winnicott, says that

> each individual is unique and the true self is an idiom of organization that seeks its personal world through the use of an object (p. 110). Thus, each person fashions life into a kind of aesthetic whose form emerges through their way of being in the world.
>
> (p. 110)

I saw a direct connection between aesthetics with mourning and loss in my creative efforts. The photographic project was at its core an act of mourning, a striving to honor "what has been lost and . . . the experience of loss itself." My own urge to create was certainly linked with an experience of death.

Hélène Cixous (1993), a philosopher and writing instructor, says that

> to begin (writing, living) we must have death . . . but young, present, ferocious death, the death of the day, today's death. The one that comes right up to us so suddenly we don't have time to avoid it, I mean to avoid feeling its breath touching us.
>
> (p. 7)

Her fondness for Kafka, whose creative writing was filled with the imaginings of torture, humiliation, disturbance, and death, is apropos to her philosophy, and she quotes him on the importance of immersing oneself in painful reading as a preparation to write creatively:

> I think we ought to only read the kind of books that wound and stab us . . . we need the books that affect us like a disaster, that grieve us deeply, like the death of someone we loved more than ourselves, like being banished into forests far from everyone, like a suicide. A book must be the axe for the frozen sea inside us.
>
> (in Cixous, 1993, p. 16)

In my view, the process of mourning requires, at a minimum, a space in which to mourn and the necessary tools that provide a connection to one's own uniqueness and to an "other" who permits and validates the poignancy of the loss. These are also the ideal circumstances for psychoanalysis to thrive. In the creation of the relational image described in this chapter, Anastasios and I became the "other" who facilitated the creative process of dealing with our losses. For me, photography created a space with the camera and the created images (and, at one time, the dark room) by which to transform loss into sight. It also became an "axe for the frozen sea inside."

Edward Weston (1924/1973) wrote that "the camera should be used for a recording of life, for rendering the very substance and quintessence of the thing itself, whether it be polished steel or palpitating flesh." I needed to counter the image of death that I had so vividly witnessed by not turning away from it but by finding prisms with which I could tolerate its presence. There is a growing literature on mourning and creativity for survivors of major traumatic events, such as the Holocaust and other genocides, which I will not be able to address in any depth here (see Ornstein, 2010; Richman, 2013). But one paper that is apropos to this discussion, by Bernstein (2000), on the visual artist Shimon Attie, links photography to creating a place for mourning. Attie's public installations, which include photographs and video, reflect on the relationship between place, memory, and identity. Bernstein focuses on Attie's project in the former Jewish section of Berlin, in which he superimposed images from old photographs depicting neighborhood life from 60 years prior. He projected these slides onto the facades of buildings that had become uninhabited shells, echoing the extermination of the Jewish population of Berlin. According to Bernstein, Attie's aesthetic helps create possible futures by not ignoring the painful past but by designing a memorial space of past and present bearing witness to the disruptive process of memory. Attie's creative imagination opens spaces for expansive play and thinking, even in the midst of devastating destruction. These are examples of relational images, new ways of seeing that involve mutual vulnerabilities, in this case of artist and viewer.

THINGS MAY NOT BE FAIR ALWAYS

All humans suffer, and we live with having to perpetually manage the anxiety of our inevitable death. Yet becoming a participant in the creation of a new relational image can help release some of the paralyzing effects of the terror of death. A musician mourns by making music, a photographer by creating an image, and a psychoanalyst-photographer by doing therapy, taking pictures, and writing about these experiences. I created a photograph that echoes Shimon Attie's photographic creations in Berlin and Aron and Atlas's (2015) "prospective function" (after Carl Jung), or the sense of constructing future possibilities from troubling repetitive impasses.

My constructed image includes me, sitting in my psychoanalytic office, with a life-size cardboard cutout of my parents behind me. The idea for the photograph

Mark Gerald, Ph.D. (and parents)
West 84th Street
New York, New York
2005 (and 1937)

was inspired by a dream in which I saw the image I went on to create. The black-and-white picture of my parents was taken from a photograph on their honeymoon in 1937. The photo of me is in color. The new blended image reunites us almost 70 years later. I derive great pleasure from this "impossible" situation. But the prospective function, while leading to hope, also points to the future and undeniable certainty of death. There it is in the photograph the reminder that we will all be together again one day. My parents' wedding song was "Always." It speaks of how life is often difficult and unfair and yet the commitment of love over time is what can be counted upon to hold a relationship together.

8 Design and architecture of psychoanalytic space

I did not immediately realize my kinship with architecture and design when I first began to photograph psychoanalysts in their offices. My initial intention was to capture a view of myself in the space in which I was spending so much of my work life. I started with self-portraits, and these provided a picture to view myself in the room in which I worked. The photographs themselves were representations of the reality of the psychoanalyst (me) in his office. But a number of years into the project, after I had been photographing other analysts in their offices and set up a website to organize the images, I began receiving emails focusing on the interiors of the rooms themselves. Architects and designers expressed interest in the work. I was interviewed on *CBS Sunday Morning* for a feature dedicated to design and decor (Osgood, 2013), invited by an online interior decorating magazine to write an article (Gerald, 2015), and written about in a number of publications catering to architects and designers. I also was approached by colleagues who shared their interest in the design and structure of their own offices. In responding to these inquiries, I realized how closely aligned some of my interests were to those in design and architecture. This deepened my appreciation for how the analytic pursuit of the psychic interior had a great deal in common with designers and architects creating livable spaces.

Models had always enchanted me. A miniature replica provides manageable entry into the overwhelmingly colossal dimensions of the world. The world I inhabited as a child, including the buildings and structures of the New York skyline, were partially accessed on subway rides "downtown" from the Bronx, visiting such monumental constructions as the Empire State Building, Radio City Music Hall, the reservoir in Central Park, and Times Square. Over the course of photographing psychoanalysts in their offices, visiting so many diverse spaces with distinctive imprints, and recognizing the common traces of Freud's shadow in each, I have come to see that these rooms, the structures that contain them, and the designs and objects found within are miniatures for the lives lived outside of the office and the dynamic interplay of analyst and patient. These spaces permit an experience of design or redesign of psychoanalytic space that is related to architectural creation and childhood building.

As a boy, I loved to visit with my upstairs neighbor Mario during the Christmas season, when his Italian-American family put up an elaborately decorated Christmas tree. Although it dwarfed the Hanukkah menorah in my family's apartment, the tree was not the object of my envy. Rather, it was the Lionel electric train set that circled the tree and induced me to get down on my hands and knees and connect with the details of the scale-model world that moved magically around the tracks in an endless loop. A few years later I got a starter set of electric trains. Over time, as I saved money received as gifts from relatives or for extra chores, I purchased additional cars beyond the basic locomotive, tender car, and caboose and added to this miniature world Plasticville buildings, including a train station with commuter figures and a large hospital.

This proto-architectural universe was a place of imagination. It afforded a welcome refuge of calm and safety from the mean streets of the surrounding neighborhood, away from the fear of being accosted by bullies or even one of the mythic gangs of the era, such as the Fordham Baldies, Italian Berettas, or Harlem Sportsmen. Playing with and building models was likewise an early activity for the prominent architect Alexander Gorlin. His elaborate boyhood creations with Legos, shown in a video as part of his presentation at a psychoanalytic forum (2013), were precursors for his award-winning work on such diverse projects as high-end residences, affordable housing for formerly homeless people, churches and synagogues, and transformations of historical sites. The architectural history of New York City featured prominently in the life and concerns of one of the subjects I photographed.

THE EVICTION OF GRIFFIN HANSBURY

"Vanishing New York," a popular blog by Jeremiah Moss, defines itself in its mission statement as "a bitterly nostalgic look at a city in the process of going extinct." This lamentation on the demise of the great city Moss imagined and found when he moved to New York from a small New England town was brought into my awareness by a friend, the fine-arts photographic printer Gabe Greenberg. He was a fan of the blog and told me I should photograph its author. It turned out that Jeremiah Moss was the pseudonym for the psychoanalyst Griffin Hansbury.

I first met with Griffin on the evening he was closing his old office and beginning to pack boxes for a move to a new place. He was leaving the St. Denis building on Broadway and 11th Street, a few blocks south of Union Square in downtown Manhattan. The timing of my visit was fraught for this analyst and blogger, described as "one of the most thorough and pugnacious chroniclers of New York's blandification" (Goodyear, 2015) and "the defender of all the undistinguished hunks of masonry that lend the streets their rhythm" (Davidson, 2017, p. 213) and who was a defender of dispossessed people and institutions on the fringes of New York. He himself was now being evicted from the 165-year-old bastion for psychotherapists of every persuasion. The denizens of the building are described in Hansbury's book, also titled *Vanishing New York* (Moss, 2018), as

> classical Freudian analysts and new-age Zen psychologists, existential counselors and gender specialists, therapists who use art, dance, and neurofeedback.

We've shared the building's six floors (plus one semi-secret half-floor on the un-seventh) with other small businesses, mostly providers of wellness – Rolfers, Reiki healers, craniosacral balancers, Feldenkrais practitioners, acupuncturists, Pilates instructors, and at least one psychic who does past-life regressions.

Standing with Griffin that night in Suite 301 at the St. Denis, I was again transported to Edmund Engelman's Austria in the dark days of 1938 Nazi-occupied Europe, in which the photographer memorialized Freud's office before his forced departure from Vienna. I felt an unease in witnessing the poignancy of this last day in a space that Griffin had occupied and felt helpless in watching it be dismantled. I also remembered my own involuntary move from the Hotel Olcott in 2004. We had agreed, since my contact with Hansbury had occurred just a day or two earlier, that I would simply visit to see what he was leaving behind after ten years of practicing in this "Great American Building" and would photograph him once he was settled in his new office.

About four months later, we met in his new office for the photoshoot. Griffin had moved from the St. Denis to the Dezer Building, about a half a mile north, which housed a hidden attraction downstairs – the Westside Rifle and Pistol Range. It seemed fitting that Griffin had landed in a space containing a strange, wondrous anomaly that spoke to a great city's capacity to hold multiple and competing views. He had exchanged neighbors of the healing arts, such as Reiki and Rolfing practitioners, for those who, in addition to shooting guns, practiced elite hand-to-hand, close-quarters combat. Yet once in Griffin's office on the second floor, there was no taint from the violent associations in the basement.

This new room was smaller than his previous office, which in addition to a consulting room, had a "back office" separated from the former by a folding screen. This "back office" is a space in most psychoanalytic offices represented simply by a desk, where the business of the practice takes place: billing, correspondence, insurance filing, notetaking, recordkeeping, and writing (case studies, theoretical papers, journal entries). It is a personal space, not an interpersonal space. Yet, like everywhere in the psychoanalytic office, this space is shared with ghosts and ancestors, with rivals and colleagues, with demons and angels.

Griffin's new office at the Dezer was a two-story structure. The tall ceiling contained a loft space with a single window, a large opening covered in a white curtain with an arrangement of pussy willows. The architectural design of the upper story seemed to invite fantasies and dreams. The window of the lower story overlooked a quintessential New York City view, not the conventional perspective framing an iconic skyscraper but a classic back-of-the building scene with an adjoining brick wall, fire escapes, and glimpses into the beauty shop across the inner courtyard. This was the kind of scene that has existed in this city for 100 years. Before television, computers, cell phones, and Netflix, people sat by their windows, sometimes conversing with their neighbors, or spying on them, or just staring into space. As much as the city has changed, here was one of the pockets of "Old New York" that had not yet vanished. In his book Hansbury quotes

Griffin Hansbury, LCSW
20 West 20th Street
New York, New York
April 28, 2018

the American novelist Sarah Schulman, who says that an apartment in New York tells many truths: "It shows where you really stand, relationally. It shows when you came, how much you had and what kind of people you knew" (as cited in Moss, 2017, p. 31). Griffin brought to his new office some of the furnishings and art that were in the St. Denis space. The loss of the previous office is poignantly felt by him. There is a feel of the authenticity of Griffin Hansbury's travels in the current room, true to his psychoanalytic vocation and to the vanishing city that sits in the enclosed back yard right outside of his window. As with Shulman's New York apartments, offices of psychoanalysts tell many truths about the office holder.

INTERIOR AND EXTERIOR ARCHITECTURES

How does the architecture and design of the spaces in which we ply our trade as psychoanalysts factor into the therapeutic equation and our professional identities? When a patient arrives for a session, what of the brick and mortar, the furnishings and décor, register in the senses and prime the flow of unconscious direction? Where in the relational matrix do synchronicity and incompatibility of aesthetic sensibilities play out in the unfolding of dialectical transferences among analyst, patient, and the shadow accomplices that inhabit the analytic office? And how important are the visual field and the physical objects that are witnesses in the psychoanalytic investigation?

In the remarkable autobiographical novel of an account of psychoanalysis, *The Words to Say It* (Cardinal, 1983), the author begins with a description of approaching her analyst's office for the first time. She describes the details of the pathway leading up to his house: "The little cul-de-sac was badly paved, full of bumps and holes, bordered by narrow, partly ruined sidewalks" (Cardinal, 1983, p. 1). She reflects upon the "mis-matched architecture" in this quiet section of Paris, which leads her to imagine who might live behind these "particular glass doors, door frames, these vestiges of decorative finish work," as she embarks on what will be a three-day-per-week, seven-year analysis. All these observations about the physical environment prepare the reader for the analytic journey of the protagonist, which traverses her own tormented body, her childhood in Algeria, and her psychological liberation.

The intersection of psychoanalysis and architecture is beautifully rendered in the writing of the New York–based architect Esther Sperber. "It is the reality of the *site*, the radical will to *incite*, and the empathic *insight* that are the transformational agents of architecture and psychoanalysis," she says (Sperber, 2014, p. 130). In emphasizing architecture as a sensual experience, Sperber (2016) notes:

> We touch, see, smell, and hear architecture. Our eyes enjoy the façade composition, our fingers brush over a cool stone sill and the warm rich fabric of the window drapery. Patterns of light and shadow punctuate the rhythmic sound of our footsteps scaling the space, measuring it against the size of our body. And

architecture stimulates our minds as present spatial experiences evoke memories of a lost past.

(p. 596)

Structures, like buildings and the rooms contained therein, are built upon a ground that previously may have housed earlier structures. The lingering effects of present and past space mingle with the expressive and receptive sensory organs of the two parties that inhabit the psychoanalytic office. Patient and therapist are primed to feel the space, through smell, touch, sounds, and sights.

Although most touching in psychoanalysis is prohibited or kept to a minimum, and the emphasis on talking-listening and thinking has been traditionally privileged, there is no explicit ban on using the other senses. Yet to look and see all that encompasses the psychoanalytic office – the buildings that these offices are part of and the furnishings and design of these psychoanalytic spaces – is to expand the realm of analysis and what is available for the exploration of the unconscious. The architect Elizabeth Danze (2005) has analyzed psychotherapeutic offices from the perspective of physical and spatial qualities, including

the couch or chair; the relative positions of the analysand to the analyst; and the design of the room itself with regard to objects, windows, views, natural light, and the sequence of entering, including the specific transition across thresholds from one space to another.

(p. 110)

The work of architect Daniel Libeskind is an example of how past experiences of design and architecture inform subsequent creations. He also expresses a kinship with the psychoanalytic understanding that every person has a history that cries out to be heard and finds its way often disguised as symptoms. Libeskind (2012) emphasizes place when he says:

History is not something which is over, which exists in the past. It is something urgent and something which is often hidden by tradition. . . . Every place has a history. Sometimes you cannot see it. The voices are almost inaudible. The actions are invisible. But yet the history continues to cry out for justice.

In a previous paper I used Leanne Domash's (2014) ideas about how architecture and design inform psychoanalysis to parse architect Daniel Libeskind's design of the Jewish Museum in Berlin (Gerald, 2014). In this paper I speculated on how early physical residences of Libeskind can be seen as model experiences for his creation of the Berlin Museum. The same influence of these model experiences can be seen in his design for the World Trade Center site in Lower Manhattan after the destruction of the original buildings on September 11, 2001. In that design, one can find an earlier creation of his as a youngster. It is a mosaic figure he built when he was at a summer camp. The camp, located in the Catskill Mountains north of

New York City, was a socialist-inspired, Yiddish cultural summer retreat for the children of Holocaust survivors such as his parents. Libeskind's figure of a partisan stepping out of the flames with a rifle and raised fist was placed next to a structure at the camp that was meant to represent the Warsaw Ghetto. Decades later, in his original design for the Freedom Tower at the World Trade Center, Libeskind came up with a sharp-angled skyscraper, topped with a twisting spire (Greenspan, 2013). His mosaic figure, created in adolescence and reaching for the sky out of the horror of Nazi atrocities, can be seen as the early model for the rising from the ashes of the proposed building at the site of the devastating attack in New York City. The final Freedom Tower design was much more subdued than Libeskind's plan, yet he felt the compromise was very close to his original idea.

Architects work by creating structures from models. These models are built to study architectural design, to discover what is possible and what needs to be changed, and to have a workable scale and materials that will allow for necessary changes. Working with a patient in a psychoanalytic office is somewhat like architectural modeling. We are not generally intervening directly in a patient's life. Rather, we are working in the realm of representation of that life. Freud's introduction of transference into psychoanalysis in 1906 furnished a model to work with, in a setting or workshop designed for the maximum expression of transference. Here is his definition: ". . . the patient sees in him [the analyst] the return, the reincarnation, of some important figure out of his childhood or past, and consequently transfers on to him feelings and reactions which undoubtedly applied to this prototype" (Freud, 1940/1949, p. 52). Freud wrote that "transference, which seems ordained to be the greatest obstacle to psychoanalysis, becomes its most powerful ally" (Freud, 1905/1963, p. 108). Since Freud's time, psychoanalysts has come to understand that these pervasive "feelings and reactions" occur in the analyst (countertransference) as well as the patient – and that this "most valuable ally" is a great guide to the unconscious minds of both parties and to the dialogue of patient and analyst in the mutuality of a therapy based on a relational model (Bass, 2015). In addition, powerful emotional responses to the environment of the entire physical–sensory realm, some in awareness and many more unconscious, are always in evidence in the psychoanalytic office. Patients and analysts use the environment of the analytic office.

While Griffin Hansbury decries the hyper-gentrification of "Old New York," with its seemingly unstoppable destruction of the character that had welcomed the marginalized of all stripes, Stefano Bolognini celebrates the enduring presence of his native city, Bologna. I photographed Stefano in June 2018, after being introduced to him by Salman Akhtar, whose generosity brought us together. Salman had been impressed with my photographs, and after I shot his office, he encouraged his friend Stefano to participate in my project.

Bologna still has many aspects of a medieval city, and its beginnings can be traced back 3,000 years. Compare this with the life span of New York, established as New Amsterdam by the Dutch in the early 1600s, about 400 years ago. The University of Bologna is considered to be the oldest university in the world.

Salman Akhtar, MD
Chestnut Street
Philadelphia, Pennsylvania
July 21, 2017

Stefano's office and that of his wife Paola, also a psychoanalyst, was a short walk from the historic center of the town. Walking in Bologna is a unique experience, in that there are miles of high portico-covered walkways that pass remnants of the ramparts that once walled in the city, numerous impressive ancient churches, and monuments of medieval, Renaissance, and Baroque art, including the twin towers that have become the iconic symbols of Bologna. The night after the photoshoot, Stefano was my guide as we strolled the streets of Bologna. I felt privileged to be introduced to the beauty of this ancient city, by a Bolognini, a true son of Bologna, whose family ties here went back many generations.

My subject's office was located in a seventeenth-century building that was part of a monastery. Stepping into the office was continuous with the awesome sense of Bologna's history and art, except scaled down to an intimate level. The walls of the spacious, high-ceilinged room were covered with drawings and paintings of old Italian masters, except for the massive bookcase that framed Stefano's desk and analytic chair. On the top of a small bookcase next to him sat a statue of the Madonna and Child. About this figure Stefano said, "It belonged to my paternal grandmother, who had inherited it from previous family generations. I had seen it from my early childhood when visiting her with my parents, so I experience a feeling of continuity when looking at it." This is an evocative object, a material thing that serves as an emotional and intellectual companion, and that can anchor memory, sustain relationships, and provoke new ideas (Turkle, 2007). The object provides this service to the analyst and serves to stimulate feelings and provoke thoughts of the patient. The psychoanalyst's armamentarium is filled with such objects. This analyst's toolbox contains all his training and experience, as well as his intellectual, emotional, conscious, and unconscious presences, and all of *that* is contained in the design of the office.

WHAT IS DESIGN?

Interior designers are interested in creating useful spaces for human dwelling and experience. This is also the concern of psychoanalysts: to create facilitating environments that can deliver an unvented or tormented self into a more mature and tranquil existence. Psychoanalytic space is the created territory in which the therapeutic work of analysis is accessed. Yet the emphasis in these two realms, psychoanalysis and design, is at opposite poles. Psychoanalysts turn inward toward the unconscious with its internal object relations. The world of design is focused on objects and appearances in the exterior domain. Actual space matters to designers. The shape, dimensions, and alignment of rooms, the furnishings contained within and adorning the grounds and boundaries of spaces, are the essential features in creating a designed space. I am intrigued and challenged in grappling with these contrasting positions and discovering areas of connection. I enter this exploration with this question: *what is design?* Since I am writing in my office, I am identified in this place as a writer. When I return to this same space with patients, it becomes transformed into a psychoanalytic office, with the particular qualities of such a space. The space defines me, and I define the space.

Stefano Bolognini, MD
Via Dell'Abbadia
Bologna, Italy
June 21, 2018

A psychoanalytic office can be a home and a sanctuary for dreams. Such spaces are associated with and conducive to dreaming with attention to lighting, comfortable chairs and a couch, wall art, and evocative objects. Privacy and quiet are present, as well as the receptive existence of the mind, ear, eye, and body of the analyst. Most psychoanalytic offices are repositories of secrets and safe spaces to be released from shame, confront darkness, and welcome dreams. A recent dream of mine contains images that reference the theme of duality I have been grappling with and additionally speaks to the symbolism of space:

> There are two structures, side by side. One is an open space, an artist's gallery in a dangerous neighborhood. There are objects of art displayed on the walls and on small tables. This artist's space was previously a garage. To enter and leave I have to duck under the heavy garage door that isn't fully open. Next to this building is a proper house, with multiple rooms, and in the strange logic of dreams, located in a more organized and safer section of town. This second construction also is involved in some form of artistic production.

Are these two edifices representative of different forms of psychoanalysis? There is much discussion in the field about how the rituals of the practice and the spontaneous moments of engagement shape and intersect with one another. Order, silence, and neutrality compete with relationship, mutuality, and uncertainty in psychoanalytic theory. Despite general agreement that both modes are valuable and inevitable, there are clusters of proponents on either side.

Yet there must be, even in the most structured, formalized version of analysis – one supported by empirical evidence of effectiveness – some degree of creative inventiveness. The artist's gallery, one that is challenging to enter (and maybe dangerous), does not guarantee an easy exit, like the door to the garage in my dream. The influential British psychoanalyst Wilfred Bion (1967) cautioned analysts to enter each psychoanalytic session without memory or desire. But what is there to protect or motivate the analyst if remembering and wanting are stripped away? Yet there is also the more proper space of analysis harkening back to that first psychoanalytic office, the workplace of Sigmund Freud. The sense of order, the frame of the 50-minute hour, exists there, even if it is illusory. The analyst occupies the analyst's chair, while the patient repairs to the couch, whether lying down or sitting, settling into the role of patient. Here is the proper house "by design."

What does it mean to design a psychoanalytic office? Freud's son Ernst was an architect who created consulting rooms for doctors and analysts, first in Berlin and then in London (Welter, 2012). Ernst Freud was commissioned to create the therapy office for the famed British psychoanalyst Melanie Klein. Some contemporary psychoanalysts hire architects and designers for the establishment of their offices. A great deal of planning often goes into the purchasing and placing of furniture and objects of art. But the real design of an analytic space is more of an organic process shaped by the ongoing influence of time and the relationships with patients, psychoanalytic forebears, and childhood homes. The action-centric model in design planning, which stresses creativity, emotion, and improvisation, in contrast to the rational model, which emphasizes planning and ordered stages, may parallel the two structures of the dream discussed above and the synergistic relationship between the "rules" of psychoanalysis and the always emerging uncertainty of actual analysis. Apropos of that convergence: while most offices I have seen and/or photographed appear to be modeled on Freud's original office, I found some notable exceptions. Sylvia Delgado's office is one example.

I met Sylvia as an advanced candidate at the Michigan Psychoanalytic Institute when I photographed her in the town of Birmingham, an affluent community of 20,000 north of Detroit. Her office, located in a walkable downtown shopping district, had modest dimensions but a strong ambience of openness. This was due primarily to two design factors: her choice of furnishings and the vastness of the slanted window that flooded the room with sky light. Sylvia was born in Lima, Peru, and lived there until her early 20s, when political and economic currents resulted in mass migration into that city and transformed it from a safe haven to a dangerous world of urban tension. Sylvia moved to the United States in 1982. She identifies herself most closely as a Mestiza (of Spanish and Indigenous background) from Lima. In spending time with her, I found her to be a blend of knowledgeable and sophisticated cosmopolitan and wise proponent of traditional wisdom. At the time of the photoshoot, she referred to her office, which she had been in for five years, as her "baby," and her patients often told her they felt "good vibes" in the room. She said she had made the place comfortable for free association.

Her choice of decor was minimalist, with mid-twentieth-century modern furniture, in the style of her childhood home, and a Mies van der Rohe couch. The couch is often the singular purchase of the new practitioner that defines their identity as *psychoanalyst* (Kravis, 2017). Sylvia explained that she bought a chair by the same high-end designer, but it was just too uncomfortable to sit in for all the hours she saw patients. She replaced the chair with the yellow one in the photo. It was a compromise for her, still not especially comfortable but at least stylish. "I like looks and style; aesthetics are important," she said. I found her attitude refreshing, and we launched into a conversation about looking and being looked at, seeing and being seen, and how these relational activities are alive for her in her work with a current patient, who looks at her all the time and brings in "body things" at the start of each session. We also talked about how these themes were alive in the photoshoot itself. The powerful need to be the object of another's gaze, and to have the freedom to look fully in return, exists in tension with the protective safety of hiding and is a dynamic that has remained underappreciated in the history of psychoanalysis.

The photoshoot, with Sylvia, myself, and my assistant, Ester, in Sylvia's office became a space for free association, and some uncanny connections arose. Sylvia and Ester (who comes from Catalonia) spoke Spanish for some part of our time together. Sylvia noted that although they never previously met, it felt as if they had known each other from another time; Ester looked like a friend of Sylvia's from her childhood. As we spoke and I photographed, another connection emerged, this time between Sylvia and me, with regard to loss. Her first analyst got pancreatic

Sylvia Delgado, MS, LLP
East Maple Road
Birmingham, Michigan
March 11, 2018

cancer and died soon after. The loss seemed sudden, and Sylvia captured something profound about the abrupt stopping of time when she said, "She will always be *my analyst who died."* Listening to Sylvia describe this breech in her life brought to my mind the unexpected and instantaneous loss of a former analyst of mine.

One day, as I was leaving a session with him, I realized I had a dream that morning about the two of us. I mentioned it, but there was no time to discuss the dream, and he said, "We can talk about it when we next meet," which would be in two days. That evening he got into a bike accident and sustained brain damage resulting in severe cognitive impairment. He never practiced again. Although he lived for another dozen years, I never returned to that office, and we never spoke of that dream. In the dream we were riding our bicycles together in the same park in which he had his accident. I often made the mistake, in subsequent years after the accident, when my therapist was still alive, of referring to the accident as "the time when he died." Sylvia commented on feeling this connection to me – of losing an analyst who goes off duty quite suddenly.

How did her office provide room for us to freely associate? Do psychoanalytic offices create an anticipation for the release of pain? Like confessionals in Catholic churches, are they designed intentionally and unconsciously to welcome loss and disturbance? Although there is no Emma Lazarus sonnet on a plaque when a patient enters a psychoanalytic office, inscribed in the office design is a welcome for the tired, the wretched, and the tempest-tossed.

Like Stefano Bolognini and Sylvia Delgado, I am the product of the city in which I was born and raised. New York's streets, buildings, and apartments, and particularly the 1950s Bronx, have and will forever be a fundamental part of my definition. The architectural soul of New York City brings this discussion full circle, back to Griffin Hansbury, who understood the power of environmental influence from an additional perspective – the lure of a beacon, calling forth a welcome for those who must escape from the limiting conditions of their surroundings. He writes (as Jeremiah Moss), "I came to New York to transition. TO BECOME A NEW YORKER after a lifetime in one small town" (Moss, 2017, p. 13). In discussing his process of urbanization and learning the rich cultural language, food, and smells of the city, he says:

> During my first years in the city, I would learn much more about passing, for I also came to New York to undergo another kind of transition. It was here that I made the passage from female to male living a queer and transgender life in the days long before Caitlyn Jenner made the cover of *Vanity Fair* and trans athletes starred in Nike commercials.
>
> (Moss, 2017, p. 14)

New York City was the place he brought his emerging self:

> I came to New York because I needed the city, and New York is for people who need cities, for those who cannot function outside of one. Open and permissive,

insulating you with the sort of anonymity you can't find in a small town or suburb, the city allows us to expand, experiment, and become our truest selves.

(p. 14)

I believe that the psychoanalytic office functions for patients in a similar way that the city functions for those who need it, as described by Hansbury and Moss. Before entering an analytic space, there is an unformulated image with associated yearning of this room where we can *become our truest selves*. And for analysts, their offices are the expression and unfolding of their professional identity as analysts.

9 The crowded office

I first met Francesca Colzani at a conference in New York City, where some of my photographs were on display. Francesca, a psychoanalyst from Chile, later invited me to a conference to be held the following year in her country – one that would involve an artistic presentation. I was intrigued by this offer, since I had never been to Chile and I liked the artistic connection. As it turned out, I had the opportunity to collaborate with her, a talented and creative artist, and we became part of each other's psychoanalytic family. Francesca's workspace is a perfect example of this chapter's topic, "the crowded office." As already discussed in previous chapters, the psychoanalytic office is a meaningful extension of the life of patient and analyst as they go about their mutually engaged work. In addition, the multiple presences found in the office often reflect a complex genealogy, both familial and psychoanalytical. Both analyst and analysand make personal contributions, bringing in those who possessed them or guided them on their journeys to the analytic room. But this discussion will focus on the analyst's presences, as well as on the complex affiliations in the history of psychoanalysis that cast deep shadows in most psychoanalytic offices.

The program in Chile focused on connections between the relational paradigm in psychoanalysis, originating in North America, and its Latin American equivalents. The conference was sponsored by the International Association of Psychoanalysis and Psychotherapy (IARPP), an organization inspired by one of the fathers of relational psychoanalysis, Stephen Mitchell. Francesca is a painter, photographer, and silkscreen artist, and we connected as psychoanalysts and artists. One project of hers involved portraits of elderly women in public squares. Francesca would photograph two subjects, apparently unrelated, sharing the same space. From the photographs she made paintings and silkscreen prints. Her images were haunting, and I was intrigued with the solitary beauty of two lost souls in each of her creations. I felt that Francesca and I were in the same field, linked in some preconscious way. It seemed we had come upon an underground matrix that gave form to something new, which created a psychic and emotional connection between us. We were both interested in people in spaces. We had a two-person show of our work at the aforementioned conference in Santiago. In writing about the show, titled "Intimacy/Variable Dimensions," Francesca said of us, "Both psychoanalysts

[are] exploring from a visual language the enigma of intimacy, the bond individuals build that sustains them in a unique space of shared experience."

MULTIPLE PRESENCES IN FRANCESCA COLZANI'S OFFICE

While in Chile, I photographed Francesca in her office. As she told me of her work and life and the history of her country, I was reminded again of how personal history and cultural context create a singular space and represent a shared sense of community. The intense light of a late summer afternoon in Santiago, in the company of Francesca Colzani, warmed "mi alma Norteamericana." I asked her to reflect upon what she saw in the photograph I had taken and to describe what her office holds for her and her patients. Her extended response speaks to the idea of numerous presences, cohabitating in the psychoanalytic space:

> Since the day I began treating patients in my office, I felt I was there by myself and in charge. I could feel the uncertainty that committing to a relationship with a new patient implied. Pretty much of what would be experienced in that space depended on how I would be able to deal with my patient's needs and capacity to engage in a therapeutic relationship. So, also from the very beginning, I paid attention to what could make me feel comfortable and secure in my own work space. I needed a well enough illuminated space with a regular and comfortable temperature (you can't take these things for granted in Chile), to begin with. And from the very beginning I understood that I needed familiar objects that would make me feel at home. Most of my furniture belonged to my grandparents or my parents.
>
> Since 2004, I am the only member of my family of origin that is still alive. When my mother died, I was 28 and beginning my private practice. I took some of the things she had given me (cushions she had embroidered, for example) to my office. I felt these things would help me feel stronger, supported by her. I also took the stones she and I used to gather in the Atacama desert. I still have them. My mother very much stimulated me in my wanting to read, study, and to be a professional, so having things that belonged to her in my office was a tribute to her and also a way to feel reassured.
>
> When my grandmother died, I also took some of the things she used everyday (little silver objects and crystal boxes, for example) to my office. I wanted her things to "charge" my office too. I noticed that the objects, which belonged to my women ancestors, made me feel more powerful, in the sense we are speaking here. I don't really know why, considering that affection came mostly from the men in my family. I have the old Parker ink pen that belonged to my grandfather, things that belonged to my father and also my brother, but they are in my mind in a different way. More like company than empowering. I also have objects given to me by patients after termination. I always see them. I think every single object in my consulting room has meaning for me. My last inclusion: the little cutlery container my youngest son gave me when he left Chile.

Francesca Colzani, Ph.D.
Santiago, Chile
November 6, 2013

So, as you can see, my office is full of all my losses. This is how I mourn, and at the same time, this is the way I still feel united to them. As I look at myself in your photo: Except that I wish I had held my hair back in a different way, I feel comfortable with the woman sitting there. I see many objects that belonged to my family, particularly to my mother, and grandmother (maternal), and presents from my daughter. I love the light coming in. Usually, I pull the curtain down a little; I need less light for psychotherapy.

This office does not resemble my analyst's or my supervisors´. Theirs were more neutral and had no objects on the furniture. I find mine more colorful and warm. Not in the photo, but on a shelf I keep books from authors that have influenced me most. To name a few: Winnicott, Bleger, Safran, Storolow, Lichtenberg, Beebe, Mitchell, Brandshaft, Benjamin, Orange. Many more influenced me, but I don't have their books. Like Paula Heiman. Mitchell is particularly important.

So my maternal family is a mystery for me. I know very little about it. My grandmother was a Lutheran, but . . . she sang songs with words in Yiddish to me. Not a word was said about where her family came from in Europe or why they came to Chile and when. Recently I had my DNA results, and 23.6% of my genes are of Ashkenazi origin. All my family on my mother's side was Jewish. So, I guess, I am an analyst, in part at least, who is honoring all those ghosts that inhabit me. Maybe that explains the deep melancholy I sometimes, during my whole life, get in touch with. Who knows?

Francesca's reflections took me on my own associative journey. I thought about how my photographs are missing the presence of patients, people who inhabit our rooms temporarily, for years or even decades. Their "absent presence" lingers as a slightly pulsating, imperceptible veil, in the space and its objects. For example, one patient of mine early in our work noticed a small object on a shelf, a miniature metal figurine of a cyclist, perhaps at Le Tour de France. Purchased in a small hobby shop on the Ile Saint-Louis in Paris, the figure wore a green jersey and black biking shorts and was riding a silver bike with one arm raised in the air, as though signaling victory. My patient was an earnest runner who used her early morning exercise in Central Park to fight encroaching despair about her inability to find a deeply loving relationship. She had many friends and an engaging career, but the room we inhabited together allowed her to express profound loneliness. The figure was somewhat aspirational for me, since I sometimes biked around the same loop in New York's Central Park as my patient ran. I was also struggling with the sense of loss caused by back pain, later diagnosed as a symptom of a tumor on my spine. For me the figure embodied the inspiration to keep fighting. In the course of therapy, the patient made significant gains and then took a long break, as her life evolved with greater intimacy. When she returned years later, to what was now a different office, she scanned the room and breathed a sigh of relief upon seeing "her guy," the man on the bike, raising his arm in triumph. This object will forever be associated with her, and her presence permanently remains in my room.

ERNST FALZEDER AND PSYCHOANALYTIC FILIATIONS

For psychoanalysts, there are additional presences in their offices besides those brought by themselves and their patients. A number of years ago, I came across a diagram by Ernst Falzeder (2005) – self-described psychologist, psychotherapist, historian, translator, skiing instructor, and pianist – containing hundreds of names in rectangular boxes, with thousands of interconnected, directional arrows and associated color coding (Falzeder, 2015). Falzeder edited for publication the correspondence between Sigmund Freud and Karl Abraham and between Freud and Sandor Ferenczi. Falzeder's map, which he called the "Spaghetti Junction," appears at first glance to be a circuit board for a complex electrical device or possibly the inner workings of a poorly planned transportation system. Upon closer inspection, it reveals itself as a creative attempt to show the history of psychoanalytic thought, through the professional relationships of psychoanalysts centered on its founder and spreading out to take into account personal influences, such as marriages, affairs, and mutual analyses. Something unique in the transmission of psychoanalytic education requires such an unusual approach in illustrating its history. Specifically, psychoanalysis necessitates a tripartite model of training which includes attending seminars and classes on psychoanalysis, receiving supervision while working with patients in psychoanalysis, and undergoing personal analysis. As Falzeder (2015) explains, "Through the personal analysis of the analyst-to-be each psychoanalyst becomes part of a genealogy, of a family tree, that ultimately goes back to Sigmund Freud and the early pioneers of psychoanalysis" (p. 51).

Before examining the value often placed by psychoanalysts on having a direct line to Freud, I will delve more deeply into the history of enmeshment, unclear boundaries, and at times crossovers into the territory of "incestuous" affairs, which characterized psychoanalysis in its formative years. My purpose is to show another aspect of the psychoanalytic office, its freedoms and constraints, and how those factors contribute to patient care. Every psychoanalyst has been a patient in their own personal analysis; many are still patients. These experiences color their own approach to working with patients. When the analyst and analysand are at work, the analyst's analyst is often there with them (Smith, 2001).

ANALYZING THE ANALYST

Most of the pioneers of psychoanalysis (those whose writings influenced future generations of analysts) had more than one analysis themselves. In a few cases, an analyst had no analysis at all. Melanie Klein was analyzed by Sandor Ferenczi and by Karl Abraham. Ferenczi was analyzed by Freud, while Abraham, like Freud, was never analyzed. These two analysts, Ferenczi and Abraham, represented differing poles of psychoanalytic theory and treatment and spawned their own significant branches of the psychoanalytic family tree. In line with Martin Bergmann's (1993) characterizations of differing contributors to psychoanalysis, Abraham could be called solid and

Martin Bergmann, Ph.D.
Fifth Avenue
New York, New York
July 21, 2003

safe, if not a particularly inspiring *extender*, whereas Ferenczi was initially a *modifier* whose contributions created controversy, even though he remained in the family fold. Subsequently, Ferenczi's ideas were viewed as a *heretical* alternative to classical Freudian drive theory. In addition to her analysis with Abraham and Ferenczi, Klein also received additional analysis from Sylvia Payne, once Klein immigrated to England, and she possibly did mutual analysis with Paula Heiman, her former analysand (Grosskurth, 1986, p. 242). Another example of multiple analyses was the case of Erich Fromm, who brought humanistic philosophy to psychoanalysis and had five analysts, including Freida Reichmann, whom he married.

EVOLUTION OF THE TRAINING SYSTEM

In thinking about these multiple personal analyses, it is important to understand the evolution of the training system of psychoanalysis (Balint, 1954). The first personal analyses, following Freud, were self-directed reflections. This early phase involved analysts thinking about themselves analytically. Of the five members of Freud's original inner circle (Ernest Jones, Sandor Ferenczi, Otto Rank, Hans Sachs, Karl Abraham), three were never analyzed: Abraham, Rank, and Sachs. The next phase of personal analysis consisted of very short sessions with Freud himself. An example of this was the case with Max Eitingon, who had only a handful of sessions, walking with Freud after dinner, over a fewer than three-week period in 1909 (Balint, 1954, p. 157). Ferenczi was the first to advocate for a much more thorough analysis for analysts and for a convergence of training analysis and therapeutic analysis. This was based, according to Michael Balint (1954), on the conviction that analysts should be at least as well analyzed as their patients.

Although each of the three parts of psychoanalytic training has individual value, personal analysis distinguishes psychoanalysis from other health professions. Specifically, physicians are not required to undergo care for various physical maladies to become a provider of such care for their patients. And social workers in training do not have to be on the receiving end of case management services before becoming certified in their profession, In distinction, there is a basic understanding among psychoanalysts that is contained in this quote from Harry Stack Sullivan (2013): "We are all much more simply human than otherwise, be we happy and successful, contented and detached, miserable and mentally disordered, or whatever" (p. 18). In other words, we are like our patients, and our patients are like us. They are in analytic treatment, and we need to have been (or still to be) in analysis, where we also bring our lives, with its joys and miseries, to another who hears (and sees).

ENMESHMENTS AND VIOLATED BOUNDARIES

The history of psychoanalysis is replete with examples of complicated relationships, in which the professional and personal position of the analyst were not sufficiently separated. And this is not just "ancient" history of the early days of psychoanalysis (see Dimen, 2011). To some degree this is an inevitable consequence of a therapy based on the importance of the unconscious in all human matters and one that is conducted in the physical privacy of the psychoanalytic office, a room dominated by the iconic couch (Kravis, 2017). Even when the patient sits in a chair and even when there is no actual couch in the room, the possibility of the couch and the implication of the couch – and its association with lying down, relaxing, and having sex (and also sleeping) creates the conditions for sex as a topic, whether that topic is addressed or avoided. I once heard that British psychoanalyst and essayist Adam Philips comment that psychoanalysis can begin when the two parties in the room agree they will not have sex. According to Falzeder (2015), many training analyses in the early years of psychoanalysis were or became erotic relationships.

When the patient and analyst are in the same profession, often members of the same training institute, and frequently in relationship with unequal power differentials, the potential for blurred, and violated boundaries is intensified. To diminish this power gap, it is typically recommended that a training analyst not be involved in any evaluative academic function for the patient-candidate. Freud saw early on that there were significant risks in this "dangerous profession" and likened the harmful effects to the handling of X-rays (Falzeder, 2015, p. 66). He recommended that because a training analysis was often short and incomplete, analysts should return periodically to analysis and do so without shame (Freud, 1937, pp. 248–249).

Adding another layer of complication to the analytic office is the early history of this profession. Falzeder's (2015) study of the analyses of psychoanalytic pioneers led him to the following observation:

> The mingling of analysis with kinship is only too clear. . . . Not only did husbands or lovers analyze each other, or were analyzed by the same analyst, not only did parents have their children analyzed by their own analysts or even analysands, but it was common practice that parents analyzed their own children, aunts their nephews, men the children of their lovers.
>
> (p. 68)

Psychoanalysis has, to some degree, cleaned up its act. But the vulnerabilities for violation inherent in the process and its arrangement remain.

THE ANALYST'S EXTENDED FAMILY

As analysts get to know their patients, they become acquainted with a vast cast of characters that compose the external and the internal world of the analysand. Current significant figures such as spouses and partners, children, friends, and work colleagues are met, and meaningful relations from childhood and the past, especially parents and siblings, are also brought into the office. The same person can exist as multiple figures, like a dominant father of the patient's childhood who is also the elderly, frail old man who needs constant care. A relatively insignificant acquaintance can make frequent appearances in the patient's dreams and represent a dynamically important theme in that person's psychological life.

Similar presences hover over the analyst. But in addition to these usual suspects, there are, as I have suggested, the many psychoanalytic relatives that are guests (some uninvited) on the analyst's side. The conventional psychoanalytic family tree or genealogy starts with Sigmund Freud, the first psychoanalyst. There is a pride, even among heretical psychoanalytic forebears (such as Otto Rank and Carl Jung), in tracing their beginnings back to the father. Jean Piaget, the Swiss psychologist who studied children's cognitive development and who was not a psychoanalyst, had a didactic analysis with Sabina Spielrein, who had been analyzed by Carl Jung. Piaget chose to emphasize Spielrein's relationship to Freud rather than to Jung, citing that she had been a student of Professor Freud's, and therefore, he, Piaget, considered himself a "grandson of Freud's" (Schepeler, 1993, p. 261).

The work of a psychoanalyst is both interpersonally engaging and lonely and isolating. Spending hour after hour with another person in the office means we are rarely alone. Yet because of the asymmetrical nature of the relationship, as seen in the payment of fees by the patient and by the focus of therapeutic attention on the patient, the analyst is the only official therapist in the room. This is true even when the analyst is deriving significant therapeutic benefits from working with a patient. This lonely and isolated position (as a solitary therapist) is countered by the arrival of professional colleagues for the analyst in the form of identifications with one's own analyst(s), supervisors, teachers, and theorists. Hearing their voices (Smith, 2001) can be comforting and/or intimidating when faced with an analytic impasse or a crisis of confidence brought up in the interactive conscious and unconscious matrix with the patient. The asymmetry in the psychoanalytic office is also balanced by the mutuality of two, all too human, partners struggling with the often devastating disturbances of life.

STEPHEN MITCHELL, PSYCHOANALYTIC FOREBEAR

This emphasis on mutuality has increased over time, diminishing the divide conventionally taken for granted by classical analysis and built into its theoretical underpinnings. Its classical view is a medical model of a physician-healer treating and curing a patient with a mental disorder. In this view there is a significant separation between self and other, between primitive functioning and a more mature approach, and between fantasy and reality. Stephen Mitchell (1998), in a paper with a deep appreciation for the overlooked contributions of Hans Loewald, helped provide an alternative to this outdated binary structure. Mitchell wrote:

> Loewald suggested [that]fantasy and reality are not experienced as antithetical to, or even separable from, each other. Rather, they interpenetrate each other. There

is a sense of enchantment in early experience, and an inevitable disenchantment accompanies the child's growing adaptation to the consensual world of objective reality. Loewald argued repeatedly that it is a fateful error, which has become a cultural norm, to mistake the world of objectivity for the true, sole reality.

(Mitchell, 1998, pp. 848–849)

I believe it is also a mistake to see the psychoanalytic office as merely an objective place for the establishment of reality and to overlook that this room where psychoanalysis takes place is a space for the interpenetration of fantasy and reality, of enchantment and disillusionment.

As Mitchell (1998, p. 849) wrote, "Those who know ghosts tell us that they long to be released from their ghost life and led to rest as ancestors." We find these ghosts in the psychoanalytic office.

Stephen Mitchell died suddenly at the end of the year 2000, at the age of 54. He had been one of my teachers during my psychoanalytic training who had an unusual capacity to bring his mind into the classroom and invite those with him to do likewise. I recall sitting in one of his seminars and visualizing a speech balloon materializing out of his head and levitating to the center of his smallish office. This spectral image represented the space his students were invited to enter and through their own creative thinking join in and deepen the conversation he had been having with himself. I took three courses with him during my time in NYU's Postdoctoral Training Program because I wanted to know psychoanalysis in the way that Stephen Mitchell taught it and wrote about it.

I never had the opportunity to photograph Stephen Mitchell in his office, since my project did not begin until a couple of years after his death. We had become friendly when we served together on the Executive Committee of the Relational Track at the University. Since we shared an interest in sports, we discussed going to a New York Knicks game. Somehow his ghost feels present to me as I write this chapter on the crowded office, and he occupies a significant space in the room where I work on Central Park West. I had a great deal of respect for him and admired his capacity to bring together disparate realms of knowledge and create a fresh perspective not previously available. As the person most credited with the establishment of relational thinking in psychoanalysis through his numerous papers, books, lectures, and teaching seminars, Steve was a beloved mentor to a whole generation of leading figures in relational psychoanalysis. One of these was Lew Aron, who I photographed in 2003.

Lew's office was located on West End Avenue between 71st and 72nd Streets. During the photoshoot, he told me that on the day he was moving in, his car was broken into, and the art that he had planned to put up on his walls was stolen. He had to find something to display and quickly purchased some nondescript paintings to take the place of what was lost. Our discussion at the time of the photoshoot was poignant because Lew was still mourning the untimely death of

Lew Aron, Ph.D.
West End Avenue
New York, New York
July 23, 2003

his dear friend and mentor. His office, in close physical proximity to Steve's office, was a room of loss. Lew explained:

> I looked for office space near his and indeed we spoke just about every day and had lunch once a week in addition to meetings and weekend get togethers. We had a study group of two in which we listened to and exchanged tapes (cassettes in those days) of various academic lectures in history and philosophy and then met to discuss them and especially to talk about their teaching style. But my fondest and most difficult memory was of walking down 71st Street each morning, and often Steve would be free at that time and we would talk through his ground floor office window. It's been almost impossible for me to walk down that block since his death. I think I must have moved in to that office somewhere around 1990.
>
> (personal communication, August 2018)

After Steve died, Lew lost his connection to his own office location, yet he remained there for another six years until he moved to his current office.

MY ANALYST'S ANALYST ANALYZED ME

Inspired by Ernst Falzeder's "Spaghetti Junction" map, I attempted to create my own psychoanalytic family tree. As I contemplated this project, I was overwhelmed with the number of people and influences that seemed to inhabit my room. First I had to establish the essential categories I would explore: analyst(s), supervisors, teachers, theorists, colleagues, office mates. There was so much data from which to choose. Where to stop? And how to handle so much material in a way that would not result in a jumble? I came across some interesting work being done using computer graphic models to present complex information. I was fortunate to meet Zannah Marsh, an interaction designer, visual artist, and programmer. Zannah had received a graduate degree in interactive telecommunications and taught data visualization at a number of colleges. Most important, she was extremely curious about psychoanalysis, was a gifted listener, and had the knowledge and skills needed to visually map information about circuitous relationships. She introduced me to the work of Edward Tufte, a statistician who has been innovative in creating designs dealing with the visual communication of information. *Beautiful Evidence* (Tufte, 2006) is an art book containing images that convey evidence and explanation. After working with Zannah and explaining the nature of various standard psychoanalytic relationships, she created a computer program using color coding: blue for analyst, red for supervisor, and so forth. Each person's name was in a node, and the nodes were connected to other nodes by lines. On the computer screen, the user could click on a node and move it about, making it closer or further away from other nodes. The program brought an active energy to visualizing the elusive and complex webs of intimacy and influence in the psychoanalytic world via its interactive map. I envision such imagery existing in the minds of all psychoanalysts and residing in a ghostlike network of their offices.

My research into my own family tree uncovered that one of my analysts had an analyst (one of three analysts he had), who was also an analyst of mine. So one of my analysts – the one I was seeing when I worked on the map – had shared a previous analyst with me. We both had seen the same analyst. I was well into my work with him when I discovered this connection. By that time, I had experienced a sense that we had things in common. My discovery that he was an artist inspired and reinforced my own commitment, evolution, and struggle with photography. There was an overlap of sensibility in our beings as psychoanalysts, fathers, husbands, and men. When I learned we had seen the same person for analysis, it seemed like more evidence of our *bashert* (Yiddish for destiny). We were meant to be together. There were also differences between us: I lived in the city, he in the country. We had different conceptions of money, and an interesting conflict arose related to that topic. I was more optimistic than he, but over time the power of his questions brought me to a deeper appreciation of the impossibilities in life. Yet I always felt him as a presence in my work, hovering around the edges of the office. We were both also collectors of things that we kept close to us in our workspaces.

He and my other analysts, and some supervisors, teachers, and colleagues provide company for me as I work with patients. They are a chorus of voices, of different registers and pitches, sometimes getting a solo, sometimes blending into a single voice of psychoanalysis. At times the voice challenges, corrects, intimidates, or coerces. But those times are more than adequately balanced with support, wisdom, humor, and love. The main players are buttressed by secondary actors, who at times take over the room. They can be friends, suite mates, or someone with whom you served on a committee or shared a panel presentation with at a conference. Such presences may even be another analyst I have heard about or the author of a paper I have read. For a while, the existence of this being can dominate the psychoanalytic space. He or she becomes a fierce competitor, critic, or idol. Together these forces counter the enormous loneliness of being a psychoanalyst, the overwhelming responsibility of absorbing so much pain, disappointment, hurt, rage, and despair.

I asked this particular analyst with whom I shared a forebear more about his psychoanalytic heritage, inquiring about the analysts of his analysts. He speculated that one of his analysts had been analyzed by Clara Thompson, who was analyzed by Ferenczi. This would place me in the Ferenczian branch of the psychoanalytic family tree. Ferenczi had a distinguished roster of analysands, in addition to Thompson and Melanie Klein. They included Ernest Jones, Michael Balint, Therese Benedek, Georg Groddeck, and Elizabeth Severn (with whom he conducted his experiments in mutual analysis). I felt in such good company. In his response to my inquiry, my analyst added:

> By the way, three great Jewish shamans in our history were Jesus, The Baal Shem Tov (Besht), and Freud – all of whom tried to heal the community, the society, the ailing populace as well as the individual. Our histories are filled with the spirits of

others who came before and held our hand while walking us through the difficult path of attempting to heal the miseries of others.

(Paul Lippmann, personal communication, August 2018)

Recently, my psychoanalytic family tree revealed a new branch, after I submitted a saliva sample to 23andMe and discovered more about my genetic ancestry. My report said I had over 1,000 DNA relatives, including 73 who were "close family to second cousins." I began corresponding with one of these relatives, a second cousin. We learned that we shared a family name. His great-grandmother was a Gershowitz, the surname of my father at birth. I realized with the thrill of discovery that they were siblings. His great-grandmother was my aunt. And then I learned as we talked that my new relative was training to be a psychoanalyst. He and I were somewhere on another family tree, one in which we share the difficult path of attempting to heal the misery of others. It is a deep comfort for me to know, as I am in my office engaged in the meaningful struggle to connect therapeutically with my patients, that I am part of a community extending back to Freud and ahead to all of the caring and gifted psychoanalytic trainees who continue to be called to this strange and noble profession.

10 A home office

Sigmund Freud's office at 19 Bergasse was a home office, on the second floor of a typical, late-nineteenth-century apartment house in Vienna's largely Jewish Ninth District. The proximity of his home and workspace has also contributed to the model of psychoanalysis that has been passed down to future generations of analysts.

We know of Freud's office not only through the photographs of Edmund Engelman and the architectural recreation of Diana Fuss and Joel Sanders (2004) but also through books and articles written by or about Freud's patients who were analyzed at 19 Bergasse (Ekstein, 1979; Grinker, 2001; Grotjahn, 1973; Wolf Man, 1958). In the book titled *Tribute to Freud* (1974), his patient Hilda Doolittle, an American poet, described approaching his office:

> I went down Bergasse, turned in the familiar entrance, *Bergasse 19, Wien IX*, it was. There were wide stone steps and a balustrade. Sometimes I met someone else coming down. The stone staircase was curved. There were two doors on the landing. The one to the right was the Professor's professional door; the one to the left, the Freud family door. Apparently, the two apartments had been arranged so that there should be as little confusion as possible between family and patients or students; there was the Professor who belonged to us, there was the Professor who belonged to the family; it was a large family with ramifications, in-laws, distant relatives, family friends. There were other apartments above but I did not very often pass anyone on the stairs, except the analysand whose hour preceded mine.
>
> (p. 3)

To enter Freud's Vienna office, a visitor had to climb a staircase, at the top of which was "a translucent interior window that look[ed] not onto an exterior courtyard but directly into the Freud family's private apartment" (Fuss & Sanders, 2004, p. 75). This interior window, which could be seen as an important prelude to each session with Dr. Freud, lent an air of uncertainty about whether one "might be on the outside looking in or the inside looking out" (p. 75). This quality of uncertainty in distinguishing the interior and exterior worlds remains one of the great ambiguities and treasures of psychoanalytic exploration and is inherent in all psychoanalytic offices.

When the psychoanalytic office is in the home, this ambiguity intensifies. Freud and his wife, Martha Bernays, had six children over an eight-year period, from 1887 to 1895. At the dawn of the twentieth century, while Freud was seeing as many as eight patients daily in his office, a brood of kids, aged five to 13, lived in close proximity – in fact right next door. Were they so well behaved and out of sight that no one on the famous couch could hear them? Did they figure in the dreams of his patients and in his own reveries as he listened for the unconscious to reveal itself? In our time a controversy exists about the ethics of even having a home office (see Gargiulo, 2007; Langs, 2007; Maroda, 2007; Mills, 2007). The concern about a home office is that the patient is overstimulated by excessive personal information about the analyst (Maroda, 2007). Salman Akhtar, whom I photographed in his office at Jefferson Medical College in Philadelphia, where he is professor of psychiatry, is one of the few analysts to have written about the psychoanalytic office (2009). He recognized that a home office, like an office outside of the home, has its advantages and liabilities. Having a window into the private life of the analyst might be overstimulating to a patient but alternately can "pull forth transferences from (the patient) that otherwise might not be evoked" (p. 115). Along with the impact a home office can have on patients, it can be a source of complexity for family members of the analyst.

JOAN WHEELIS AND THE LATTICE WINDOW

Joan Wheelis has written a memoir (2019) of what it was like growing up with parents who were both distinguished psychoanalysts and living in the house in which they practiced. Her experience provides a unique perspective on some of the nuances and complexities of the home office:

> There were five floors from the street level of garage and wine cellar and 63 steps to climb to reach the main entrance. Patients climbed the first 17 steps to the first turn where there was a blue door. My parents buzzed in their patients through this entry. The waiting room was immediately to the left of another flight of internal stairs. If they were going to see my father, he would walk out of his office and stand at the top of the stairs, the noise of double doors opening alerting the patient in the waiting room that he was ready. My mother would buzz again for her patients, who would climb the same steps to my father's office and then at the landing open the orange door of a two-person elevator. From there the patient traveled past the fourth floor of our house where the living room, kitchen and dining room were and finally to the top floor where my mother's office and our bedrooms were. Separating the house from her office was a three-inch solid oak door.
> (pp. 26–27)

Joan discovered in this great Victorian building, home to her and her parents and a work environment for the adults, a small storage area with a wooden lattice opening which looked directly at the door of her father's office. This secret space, in which she could see who came to her father's door, filled her with feelings of excitement in violating a prohibition. Young Joan, a big fan of the book series *Harriet the Spy*, had a portal into the professional life of her father.

Psychoanalytic practices have a rhythm that is measured in time, which young Joan realized at an early age. Her father emphasized this essential part of psychoanalysis in the description of an analytic office in his novel, *The Doctor of Desire* (1987).

> High ceilings, two pairs of French doors opening onto balconies. A beautiful room. Large, light, elegant. Polished teak floors, antique Caucasian rugs. A Klee drawing, Man on a Tightrope. Two walls of books, the multi-colored spines a clamor of contending voices and visions, confined to order by solid walnut shelves. And clocks, clocks everywhere, of an accuracy so far exceeding his need as to become a celebration of time, the commodity he sells; he could no more do without clocks than a greengrocer his scales. . . . The clocks measure out the listening into 50-minute hours, the longing is continuous, flows on forever.
>
> (A. Wheelis, 1987, p. 16)

Joan was hyper-aware of her parents' time and their patients' comings and goings (J. Wheelis, 2019, p. 29):

> My father wrote in the morning and then saw five patients after lunch, from 1:30 to 6:20, with ten-minute breaks between them. My mother saw patients all day starting at 8:10 (9:00, 9:50, 10:40, 11:30). Her breaks were the couple of minutes it took for one patient to leave by the elevator and the next to take the elevator up. At 12:20 she joined my father for lunch and then went back at 1:20, ending her day at 6:20.

Although patients in some home office arrangements may be able to decipher the difference between "the Professor who belong(s) to us and the Professor who belong(s) to the family," members of the analyst's family may require more vigilance to make and keep that distinction.

Joan captures some of the complex intimacy in the relationships between family members and patients in her description of a particular patient. Even when there are good boundaries kept by analysts in protecting the privacy of their patients, family members are aware of the specialness of patients in the lives of their parents. This experience became a turning point for Joan (J. Wheelis, 2019, pp. 30–31):

> My parents never discovered my spying. But shortly before I stopped my undercover reconnaissance, I was startled to recognize a famous pop singer coming up the stairs with her guitar to see my father. She had been an idol of mine and I could hardly believe that I had seen her from just a few feet away, let alone then listened to her sing and play guitar from within my father's office. The exquisite

Allen Wheelis, MD
Jackson Street
San Francisco, California
February 25, 2004

Joan Wheelis, MD (with her parents)
Garden Street
Cambridge, Massachusetts
September 21, 2004

pleasure of the discovery was intoxicating. The subsequent guilt, however, was even more overwhelming and I forever abandoned my post at the lattice window.

I first learned about Joan after shooting Allen Wheelis in San Francisco. He suggested I also photograph his daughter, Joan, an analyst in Cambridge, Massachusetts. Eight months later, I met Joan Wheelis in her home office on Garden Street. Allen and Joan's psychoanalyst mother Ilse were visiting at the time, and I managed to get a family photograph.

CONVENIENCE AND ENCLOSURE OF THE HOME OFFICE

A home office can provide a sense of continuity for the analyst and has the additional benefit of eliminating commuting and the extra cost of renting or purchasing additional space in which to practice. A home office unites important parts of a practitioner's life and counters the split separating the personal from the person at work. However, given the issues that can arise with a home office, there is good reason to attend to the practitioner's motivation for having a home office and the impact of that arrangement on patients as well as on the analyst's family. Psychoanalysts are mental health professionals and as such are guided by "do no harm"; at the same time psychoanalysis is part "art," and how the analyst-artist lives their life is an important part of their essence as an analyst.

It was not until the end of the 1700s that the domestic interior became separate from the place of work (Bell, 2013). But this separation – often with the implied gendered designation that home was inescapably feminized space while the work office was the male domain – was never absolute. Home itself was often a combined space. The British architect Frances Holliss (2012) has coined the term "workhome" to describe this important type of building. However, what was once common practice (for example, the English longhouse, combining livestock work and human dwelling in the same single-storied rectangular building, or dwellings in which merchants and crafters lived and manufactured goods under the same roof) went out of fashion by the 1950s, when housing-development rules prohibited home-based work. Nonetheless, Holliss (2012) gives numerous examples of the persistence of workhomes in architectural history, which included those of artists, craft workers, and professionals.

A prime example of a workhome is the Maison de Verre, built in Paris in the early twentieth century. Its ground floor consisted of consulting rooms for a gynecologist, with two floors of living accommodations for the doctor and his family above. Dr. Jean Dalsace worked and lived in this house. An active member of the French Communist Party, he hosted celebrated Marxist thinkers of the time in the second floor salon of the "Glass House," so-named because of the prominent use of glass in the building's architectural design. In the 1930s, poets, painters, sculptors, film makers, and philosophers were all, at one time or another, guests in the upstairs salon of Jean and Annie Delsace (Delistraty, 2017). Walter Benjamin was impressed with the building, viewing it as an anticapitalist, utopian, "culture of glass": "that glass is such a hard, smooth material to which nothing can be fixed. A cold and sober material into the bargain. Objects made of glass have no "aura." Glass is, in general, the enemy of secrets. It is also the enemy of possession" (Benjamin, 1933, pp. 733–734).

The layout of the psychoanalytic workhome often locates the work office on the ground floor and the living quarters upstairs. When I lived in Southern California in the 1970s, I attended sessions with an analyst in his dream house in the foothills of Montecito, just east of Santa Barbara. His modest home with its beautiful scenic view in one of the wealthiest communities in the United States was, ironically, a reminder of his childhood home. He had grown up living above the family business, a butcher shop, in an immigrant section of Chicago. The incongruity of these two disparate locations was somehow overcome by the link of having his life of work and family all under one roof.

ANALYSTS' HOME OFFICES

About a third of approximately 100 analysts I have photographed practice from a home office. These settings have been in townhouses, apartments, and suburban homes. Some offices have been separate buildings on the home property, others have had designated entrances for patients, and some more intimately share space with the living quarters of the analyst. Each office is revealed in its photograph as a distinctive space containing the analyst and their personal accoutrements, and each office reveals the profession of psychoanalysis itself.

Nechama Liss-Levinson on the ground floor
Nechama works out of her home office in Great Neck, an upscale suburban town in the metropolitan area of New York. She built her office when her kids went off to college, with a separate entrance, full bathroom, and its own waiting room. The office suite was conceived as a space that could also serve as guest quarters for her married children and eventual grandchildren, so it included a bathroom. Nechama, thinking forward, also envisioned the ground floor as a place to live when she and her husband could no longer climb to their second-floor bedroom.

Not surprisingly, Nechama Liss-Levinson exhibits a great deal of groundedness. Akhtar (2009) wrote about what he believes is a real, albeit subtle, connection of ground-floor offices to the nonhuman environment and to deeper connections. "The ground under one's feet lends itself well to being equated, in the unconscious phantasy, with the reassuring strength of parental bodies and their holding functions," he explains (p. 116). The influence of Nechama's parents can be seen in myriad objects in her home office and in family photos in her adjacent living quarters. Nechama saw her patients in a number of spaces, sometimes under difficult circumstances. Her first "office" was the third bedroom in the apartment she shared with her husband and newborn. While her husband was putting their daughter to bed, Nechama would often see patients. Sometimes the baby would be fussy, and no matter how far from the "office" Nechama's husband would take her, she still could hear the baby crying: "It was awful. I was still nursing and could feel the milk coming in when she cried. Definitely not a good situation for me or my patients!"

Nechama shared her second workspace, a tiny, enclosed, underground room, with a physical therapist. The room could accommodate only two chairs and a small table, but somehow it felt bigger to her than her previous home office. When the physical therapist decided not to renew their lease, Nechama felt devastated. For the psychoanalyst, not having a space to practice is like a soccer player not having a ball. You cannot be your (analytic) self without an office. The loss of this office served as a catalyst for her to find a better space and begin a full-time practice, which required a leap of faith. Psychoanalysts in private practice often experience going solo as a crisis because of the inherent risks in beginning any independent business, as well as those risks peculiar to the psychoanalytic trade. How will I get patients? Where can referrals come from? How do I manage the business aspect? What is an appropriate fee? What happens when a patient doesn't show up for an appointment? Can a fee once set with a patient be increased over time? Do the benefits of being on approved insurance panels for in-network practitioners outweigh the liabilities? These are the fraught questions that arise when going it alone.

Early in her psychoanalytic career, Nechama addressed the often neglected topic of money through the prism of the equally minimized topic of being a woman analyst. In "Money Matters and the Woman Analyst: In a Different Voice" (Liss-Levinson, 1990), she described a woman's struggle with setting fees and the complex issues pertaining to female desire. In honoring the complexity of such essential struggles and referencing the work of Jessica Benjamin (1988) on what became the centrality of mutual recognition in psychoanalysis, Nechama wrote:

> What happens, I wonder, when we attempt an intersubjective viewpoint? To whose needs are we attending? When we accommodate to the needs of the other, what gets pushed aside and out of our awareness – the anxiety of saying no, the reality of one's lack of compassion, the awareness of ourselves as separate from our patients? Are we sure it is the needs of our patients we are hearing or is it our own needs, speaking rather loudly and overwhelming our senses? Is an emphasis on the needs of the other a symptom of money-blindness, an analytic error in gratifying the needs of the patient, or possibly . . . a woman speaking in her own voice, or hearing more clearly the voices of others?
>
> (Liss-Levinson, 1990, p. 129)

Nechama's home office was thoughtfully designed for recognition of the mutual needs and desires of her patients and herself. The walls are painted in "healing aloe," and gifts of small objects patients gave her are meaningfully integrated into the office design. Landscape photographs taken by Nechama during her travels are hung on the walls, and on the floor are two sculptures symbolizing the analytic journey. She installed a fireplace in the office, linking back to the one she vividly remembered from the office of analyst Susan Lowenstein, a character

Nechama Liss-Levinson, Ph.D.
Church Street
Great Neck, New York
November 4, 2018

in *The Prince of Tides* movie. "In practice, the fireplace makes the room very hot, very quickly," Nechama said. "But sometimes, on a really freezing cold day, or when I just think it works with the work we are doing, I turn the fireplace on (it's gas) and things begin to cook" (personal communication, October 20, 2017).

Craig Polite in the city

Craig Polite was the discussant in May 2017 on the work of Kirkland Vaughans and Warren Spielberg, the authors of *The Psychology of Black Boys and Adolescents* (2014). Craig gave the requisite review of each of the author's papers with an emphasis on their strengths. He cited his personal recognition of the pain inherent in racism and how Black boys are often seen as being older than they actually are, leading to a tendency for White people to fear them and treat them as adults. And Craig described how, as he was reading these significant papers, he became gripped by a creeping anxiety and realized, "Oh my God, this is the story of my life!" He then spoke poignantly of his experience growing up in Queens, New York, and living with the pressures of making it in a White world. Managing to be both good and cool left him living on a knife's edge, where there was always the risk of annihilation. Sitting in the audience at this meeting of psychoanalysts and listening to the rare testimony of someone who experienced the life-and-death impact of racism, I felt the powerful impact of this man's openness and vulnerability.

Craig and I had been colleagues for many years, but we began to socialize only about ten years ago, when we met occasionally for dinner at a Thai restaurant. I had always seen Craig as an extremely comfortable member of our psychoanalytic community, especially at social gatherings. Our Institute at New York University, since its founding in 1961 by Bernie Kalinkowitz, had long recognized the importance of bringing diverse voices into analysis. But it was not uncommon that at many Institute events, Craig was either the only analyst of color or one of a few. The pressure of living on the knife's edge became vividly clear in Craig's sharing his struggle. In 1992, he co-authored the book *Children of the Dream* (Edwards & Polite) and said in the introduction:

> For whatever successes blacks have achieved are the results of battles hard fought and hard won, the legacy of many thousands gone who lived and died fighting to ensure that their children would "live to see a better day" – that, in the words of the prophet who had a dream, "little children will one day live in a nation where they will not be judged by the color of their skin but by the content of their character." These are the children of the dream.
>
> (p. 8)

Craig is part of Black Psychoanalysts Speak, a group that has created a film and periodically presents it at many psychoanalytic forums. The film challenges psychoanalysis to live up to its unrealized promise as a progressive movement devoted to the common good. The group challenges audiences to grapple with issues of race, culture, and class and to open the profession and its clinical gifts to more people than just the privileged. I am privileged to have Craig Polite as a colleague and friend, to be inspired to grapple with the destructiveness of racism and the inequities that permeate society and affect all of us, and to have had the opportunity to create a relational image of him in his office.

Craig's workspace is on a busy commercial street in the Midtown East section of Manhattan. The building is a postwar condominium, whose ground floor is occupied by a popular Chinese restaurant. Craig has a one-bedroom apartment in the building in which he sees patients and also lives in during his three-days-per-week practice. His workplace in the city reflects a commonality of many psychoanalytic offices. The greatest concentrations of psychoanalysts and psychoanalytic patients are in major cities in North and South America, Canada, Mexico, and Europe. There are also thriving psychoanalytic enclaves elsewhere in the world, often associated with centers of training at universities or stand-alone institutes. But on the whole, urban centers are highly correlated with psychoanalysis. Perhaps its origin in the great cosmopolitan center of Vienna accounts for the recreation of zones of analysis in cities throughout the world. Buenos Aires, which may have the highest per capita number of analysts in the world has a neighborhood called "Villa Freud," containing a large number of therapists' offices. It makes sense to have a psychoanalytic practice in a city, since that is where paying patients live.

I photographed Craig two days after Christmas in 2016, when a red neon holiday decoration was still reflecting in the window of his office. We took some photographs in that part of the apartment adjacent to the window and then moved into the space with a large wall mirror. In this section of the apartment, Craig sat in one leather Stressless chair, while an identical seat for the patient was catty-cornered and separated by a low wooden table with a lamp. Prominently displayed on the wall was a drawing of an African couple that showed a caring, grooming gesture being given and received. The man wears a Basotho, or blanket scarf, with a design of flowing lines of orange and grey. This pattern is mirrored in the rug on the floor, where the colors undulate even more. When I asked Craig about what he saw in the photograph, he emphasized the caring relationship in the drawing – people being at ease with one another. He added that the room reflected his own flow, the sense that a patient need not get flustered, that "we will work this out."

Aisha Abbasi among the trees

Aisha's home office is in West Bloomfield, Michigan, in the greater Detroit area. Metro Detroit has one of the largest settlements of Middle Eastern people in the United States, including Jews, Assyrians, Chaldeans, and Arabs. Aisha was born and educated in Pakistan. She traced her comfort with a home office to her childhood, when her mother, a physician, practiced in a hospital that was out the door and down a corridor from their home outside of Islamabad. But despite great warmth and one of the most infectious and genuine laughs I had ever heard, she

Craig Polite, Ph.D.
East 55th Street
New York, New York
December 27, 2016

Aisha Abbasi, MD
Bloomfield Glens
West Bloomfield, Michigan
March 11, 2018

has had her share of early trauma, resulting from the partition of India and Pakistan in 1947 and the Indo-Pakistan war of 1965.

Upon entering her office, I was stuck by the view from the multiple bow windows looking out on her yard. On this bright winter day, with snow on the ground, the windows provided a view of a large, sturdy tree with a tire swing hanging from its branches, which foregrounded the wood area behind it. Aisha said patients often responded to the view, which had become part of her therapeutic repertoire. She explained, "This is an old maple, and it's taken a few hits." When a patient has a fear of dependency, she says, "You have to put your roots deep in, before you can stand up like that, and then you can take a few hits and survive."

The wars during her childhood provided some hits to Aisha's family. Her father was a colonel in the Pakistani army and was injured in the first conflict, when she was four years old. She remembers that there was shelling every night and bunkers in the yard that they had to run into for shelter. During the Indo-Pakistan War, her father was captured and spent three years in an Indian prison. Her office honors her Pakistani heritage in the design presence of several arches, reminiscent of Muslim architecture. A reflection of one of these arches on the floor can be seen in the photograph.

Having a home office proved complicated after the World Trade Center attacks. Patients coming to her home got glimpses of family members, including her husband Aamer, and some clients reacted to their brown skin and "Middle Eastern look." One patient said, "I don't know which side you're on." Another patient, who had always paid reliably, began withholding payment. When Aisha asked her what was going on, the woman replied that she was embarrassed to say she did not want to give Aisha money because she felt if might be sent to fund Al-Qaeda. Redefining herself against the background of American culture and dealing with these later clinical impasses caused by unfounded prejudice has been an ongoing process for Aisha. She is a Muslim who celebrates her culture and Muslim holidays but who has moved away from observant religious practices. She made the opposite journey, however, regarding traditional Pakistani clothing. Originally she was uncomfortable wearing the traditional *shalwar kameez*, composed of baggy trousers, a long blouse, and a scarf, and she also didn't wear dresses to work.

Then, sometime during her first analysis, she started wearing dresses, coinciding with her mother's illness in Pakistan. Aisha was traveling back and forth from her homeland in Pakistan and her home in America, where she and her husband had created a new life, with children and careers. She remembered in this movement between cultures that she started to feel more comfortable in both places. She would look at her clothes in her closet in the morning and choose from those, Pakistani or Western, that represented how she was feeling that day. Her varied wardrobe reflected all of her, and wearing the *shalwar kameez* helped her feel connected to her mother.

Spending time photographing Aisha Abbasi in her home office felt full. She gave much of herself, and I felt the therapeutic benefits. She shared the loss of

Dale Boesky, MD
Watkins Street
Birmingham, Michigan
March 10, 2018

her parents and how being able to work out one's issues with parents is severely curtailed when a parent dies early in a child's life. Aisha's generosity and intuitive ability were evident from when we first began to communicate through email about the photoshoot. She asked me if I would photograph Dale Boesky, a highly respected analyst at the Michigan Psychoanalytic Institute, where Aisha is on the faculty. Dale, close to 90, was Aisha's analyst, and she is grateful to him for all she accomplished in her years of analysis (three significant segments of work over a 20-year period). During that same weekend in March 2018, I photographed Dale in his home office in Birmingham, Michigan.

Along with the many gifts I received in that weekend in Metro Detroit was the way Aisha captured the importance of integrating the visual into psychoanalysis. She said, "The seeing cure is in natural alignment with the talking cure." In her office, there were some small metal sculptures on a shelf beneath the windows. One was a girl on a swing, purchased by Aisha in Boston, where she did some of her training. She connected the object to her girlhood, and it also resonated with the tire swing on the old maple tree in the yard that had taken its share of hits. There are some home offices that truly makes one feel at home. Aisha's office welcomed me and my camera with warmth and generosity.

11 Retaining the shadow in changing times

The experience of photographing psychoanalysts in their offices has focused my attention on the historical meaning of our workspaces, their current significations, and how they may shape up in the future. I have photographed almost 100 analysts in their offices in North and South America and in Europe. I have photographed major figures in the field, candidates at institutes, and a wide range of professionals practicing varying types of psychoanalysis. They have generally welcomed the opportunity to be seen, regardless of theoretical orientation. All work in that special province that is the psychoanalytic office, all are office holders of psychoanalysis, all toil to clarify and alleviate the suffering of others, and most all are shaded to some degree by Freud's couch.

Following Freud's first psychoanalytic office, we have carried forward traditions of filling our surroundings with objects and maintaining a precarious hold on the permanence of space. So what does the history of the psychoanalytic office portend for the future of our profession? The Jungian *temenos* (Abramovitch, 1997, 2002), or secure continuous containment, is under siege. Technological advances and the frantic pace of modern life will provide new opportunities, challenge assumptions, and even call into question the necessity of having a psychoanalytic office at all. Finding a space where we can belong, with our belongings, may define and predict our future existence.

As analysts, we listen and sometimes hear. We see and sometimes notice. And with the partnership of an "other" (our patient), we can be heard, and we can be seen. Looking at ourselves is not to be taken for granted. It is a physical act that is impossible without the assistance of a mirror or a camera. Yet, as the great environmental portrait photographer Arnold Newman (2000, p. 21) said, "We do not take pictures with our cameras, but with our hearts and minds." When I began this project, I wondered if my psychoanalytic colleagues would agree to have their picture taken and potentially displayed in a book. I started with a self-portrait. How did I look in my workspace? What was it like to be the central subject rather than primarily the observer? At first, it felt a little awkward but also interesting. I was both a familiar and a new object. I followed by asking my closest analyst friends to be photographed, hoping our friendship would allay any inhibitions to participate.

As the project evolved, I asked others – seeking a representative sample of the changing face of psychoanalysis in the new millennium. I wanted, in addition to both senior and junior members, to portray the increasing presence of women, people of color, of varying ethnic backgrounds and sexual orientation, and people of different nationalities (limited, of course, by my travel budget). I received an enormous, positive response among the people I asked, and rarely did someone turn me down. This reaction challenged the stereotype I had first heard in my own psychoanalytic training – that analysts are essentially antisocial. The changing climate in psychoanalysis – away from the orthodox view of seeing the analyst as an objective instrument and toward seeing the analyst as someone who creates a relational, intersubjective framework that recognizes the all-too-human analyst himself or herself – likely played an important role in my subjects' willingness to be present with me and my camera. Sometimes analysts contacted me to tell about their own or another's office that was noteworthy for its design, the climate it created, or some special feature that should not be missed – a handmade psychoanalytic couch, a spectacular view, a rare collection. This confirmed for me that a professional office is so much more than simply a workspace, but rather, is a created area in which the deepest wishes and darkest fears could be revealed, held, and explored.

When Edmund Engelman entered Bergasse 19 in May of 1938, the Freuds were scheduled to leave for London in ten days. Engelman worked for two days photographing every nook and cranny:

> I entered and had my first glance of the famous couch; it was relatively small. Antiquities filled every available spot in the room. I was overwhelmed by the masses of figurines which overflowed every surface . . . the couch itself was covered with an Oriental rug and pillows piled high on it, so that it seemed a patient lying on it would almost have to sit up. The walls were covered with pictures, pieces of art, mementos, and awards . . . wherever one looked, there was a glimpse into the past.
>
> (Engelman, 1976, pp. 96–97)

This study has explored how the original office has influenced contemporary psychoanalytic spaces throughout the world: rarely does a psychoanalyst's office not have a couch, analyst chair, bookcases, art, objects, and mementos. Edgar Levenson, an interpersonal analyst, may speak for many contemporary practitioners when he said, "I don't use the couch [in my practice with my patients], but if I did not have a couch, I would not feel like an analyst" (personal communication, October 7, 2003). As is evident from the photographs, in addition to standard psychoanalytic design, each office has a distinctive expression of the analyst's individuality. Personal tastes, cultural influences, economic circumstances, and histories are reflected in the choice of colors, light, furnishings, office size, and neighborhood and whether the office stands alone, in a home or commercial workspace, or as part of an institution. These factors combine to produce a dialectic of operating within the community of psychoanalysis, with all its history, and having a unique presence. And this tension is essential in keeping the field vibrant and available for adaptation and growth.

Edgar Levenson, MD
West 72nd Street
New York, New York
October 7, 2003

Psychoanalytic spaces today still provide a glimpse into the past, despite technological changes, and remain repositories of our patients and our own inner worlds. We carry a storage room of memories from all the homes in which we have lived. Inhabited space comes to inhabit us, and in this regard, we are all transients, wayfarers, dust-bowlers, homeless souls traversing a world in which we seek familiar and safe terrain in which to unpack our belongings and rest in a peaceful, if only temporary space, in harmony with the world. In photographing analysts in their workspaces, some expressed a casual nonchalance or stated disinterest in the meaning represented by their physical environment. On a number of occasions, when I asked my subjects what was behind them, they turned to look before answering. When I would ask about a painting or photograph or arrangement of books in their background, it became apparent, however, that there was an important self-expression in these objects and designs. What is behind us is the way we are framed, how the analyst is contained, what is chosen as the holding environment for the work. Much more can be said about the chair we sit in and other aspects of our workspace and their objects. All of these reflect how we present to the world and who we are in our work with patients. Related to this is how our bodies, clothing, hair styles, and facial makeup (including variations in facial hair design for men) create a significant expressive home for our analytic selves. It is more common today, and I predict will be increasingly so, for analysts and, of course, patients, to express themselves with body art, jewelry, and hair coloring.

It is necessary to have, in our homelike workspaces a sense of privacy, a feeling of safety and belonging, and an asylum for self-definition away from the world that demands our attention and can threaten access to the deep regions of the unconscious, with its living terrors and the creative powers to transform pain into language, into healing, into art. This seems not only true for our patients but also, since many of us spend so much time at work, for we analysts. The longing for a home, to return home, is an organizing and universal narrative (Seiden, 2009). To yearn for a sanctuary and struggle against the inevitable acceptance that you can't go home again is a central theme in analysis, even when the ideal home is a fantasized corrective to an origin that is steeped in pain, poverty, and trauma (E. Gerald, personal communication, January 12, 2010). Our offices can provide a ballast against the life forces that require the leaving of home and the resulting alienation and feeling of being a stranger in a hostile world. Psychoanalytic offices are inviting places. The patient's first experience of analysis is often the sensory impressions of entering the inner sanctum. Adam Gopnik (1998) described such an encounter in his story, "Man Goes to See a Doctor":

I've read that you're not supposed to notice anything in the analyst's office, but that first evening I noticed it all. There was the couch, a nice Charles Eames job. On the wall there was a Motherwell print – a quick ink jet – and, opposite, a framed poster of one of the Masaccio frescoes in Santa Maria del Carmine in Florence. I was instantly impressed. The two images seemed to position him (and me) between Italian humanism, in its first, rocky, realistic form at one end, and postwar New York humanism, in its jumpy, anxiety-purging form, at the other. On a bookshelf beside him were nothing but bound volumes of a psychoanalytic journal, rising to the ceiling. . . . He was lit by a single shaded bulb, just to his left. . . . This put his face in a vaguely sinister half light, but . . . the scene had a comforting European melancholia.

(p. 20)

For Jungian analysts, healing is seen as composed of both the relationship and the space. Some Jungian analysts, like Andrew Samuels, whom I photographed in London in 2005, have an office in a building's interior, which add to the environment's internality. What happens to this sacred space when a move or change threatens to disrupt? When there is the disruption of change, the healing pact can be broken for either party, and *temenos*, that secure continuous containment, is lost (Abramovitch, 1997). I have discovered that, for many analysts, the sense of secure containment an office represents has not been continuous in their careers. There have been moves, sometimes desired and sometimes the result of external pressures. Many analysts split their work lives into more than one location. Some have institutional as well as private offices. Freud himself suffered the trauma of moving house. A few months after leaving Vienna, he wrote from the security of exile in London:

All our belongings have arrived undamaged, my collection has much more space and looks much more impressive than in Vienna. [Nonetheless,] . . . the collection is dead now, nothing is being added to it any more, and [it is] almost as dead as its owner.

(Engelman, 1998, p. 21)

As we look to the future, it is essential to the survival of psychoanalysis that we analysts maintain a sense of vibrancy, an ability to thrive in an ever-changing world. In photographing and interviewing my colleagues, I found the profession in the early twenty-first century to be very much alive. Yet we are in a great period of upheaval, uncertainty, and transition. Much has been written and discussed about the proliferation of psychopharmacology, competing short-term and less costly therapies, and frustration with the slow pace of analysis. Concerns about the future of psychoanalysis have existed from its genesis, and, to quote Mark Twain, reports of its death have been greatly exaggerated. Yet it is essential to struggle with how to protect the precious attentiveness to inner life that psychoanalysis is concerned with. The heart and mind of psychoanalysis survived its move from Vienna and was not only carried throughout the world but also adapted to the cultures and climate of rapidly changing environments. It was also vividly experienced in the innumerable recreations of Freud's office, with their design and objects providing a space for the generativity of our work – and a home for ourselves.

Nonetheless, the frenetic pace of technological change has altered the fundamental process of analysis, which threatens the private in favor of the public

Andrew Samuels, Ph.D.
Mercers Road
London, England
August 8, 2005

(Goren, 2003). Can we preserve the psychoanalytic space of secure continuous containment when that experience is increasingly rare and increasingly expensive? The use of telephone sessions and video communication, such as the Skype platform, necessitated by the fluid demands of modern life, have become more commonplace, even in psychoanalysis. Dale Boesky, a senior analyst in Michigan, told me of starting a recent analysis with a patient entirely on Skype. He said he had reservations about using the new technology for five minutes but became convinced of its being a viable means of treatment for the same reason that most analysts decide to work in analysis with most analysands, "because she was a wonderful patient" (personal communication, March 10, 2018).

It is not always necessary to be in one's office to conduct a session on the phone or by computer. But how do we belong as psychoanalysts, if our offices, with their collections of belongings, cease to be our exclusive place of work? The usual objects that are associated with our defining sense of ourselves are not always present if we work from locations that are remote from our offices. Now and in the future, our entire relationship to objects may need to be revisited. The word object for analysts connotes both an external item and, more important, the internalized representation of a person, a relationship, or a fragment of such person or relationship. External objects tend to be important because they can evoke the memory, emotion, and sense of an other in one's life. This capacity for rich and stable object relations is often tantamount to a flexible, creative, empathic, and receptive mental well-being. For each of us, certain material objects are especially evocative (Turkle, 2007).

When analyst and patient occupy the same physical space, there is a shared array of physical things to which either may respond. In observing and commenting on a piece of art in the office, for example, a patient may be reminded of a dream. The analyst, in the presence of this same piece of art, can through reverie join the patient in the unconscious joint construction of the analytic third (Ogden, 1994). How is the space for analytic work co-created when the means of connection is facilitated and experienced through electronic communication? What happens when the patient is in a hotel room in Beijing, where it is midnight, and the analyst is sitting in his or her office on the Upper West Side in New York City at 11 in the morning? Each is contained in a separate environment, responding in subtle ways to their own personal enveloping and interactive space. This new arrangement requires attention to the details of the different rooms (or even outdoor spaces) that patients and analysts occupy. On the telephone, it may be useful to reflect upon or inquire about where patients are situated. What is the nature of their space? What objects are present? What are they facing? What is behind them? Are they seated, lying down, standing, pacing the room? Are they aware of your space? How do they picture the analyst?

Video-enhanced sessions, compared with telephone sessions, allow for some greater experience of the other's *temenos*. These sessions usually include a picture within the picture, in which therapists can see themselves on a smaller screen – the way patients are seeing them. The patient, on the other end of the connection, is also faced with this dual view. I have had these sessions in which patients, using laptop computers, have carried them around their room, revealing the space they are occupying, the environment that may be occupying them. These advances can be exciting, opening up many more possible ways of working when patients are traveling or have moved far away. At the same time, these changes can be destabilizing. In order not to die, we must protect a space – in ourselves and in interaction with a secure *temenos* that welcomes and nurtures our deeply intimate and creative work. The struggle to hold onto our home, knowing that it is under siege and inevitably will be lost, is one of the profound challenges we face as human beings. It may be necessary, as in some way it has always been, to take possession, occupy and fill our offices with ourselves and our belongings, in the trust that this space will create, protect, and nurture our future, even if we are the only occupant in the room.

Good analytic work always requires a dialectic tension between the security of a framework of rules and the freedom to wander about in the created space that the analytic office represents.

Analysts are currently challenged to exercise a discipline to remain in their analytic home, the office, and continue to refurbish this space with new, meaningful objects. This may involve developing a relationship with technological means of communication so that the phone, and especially the computer, become available as evocative instruments in our new psychoanalytic spaces. Even when the psychoanalytic office changes in shape and content and becomes a virtual space, it can always be a refuge for the unconscious if we allow the shadow of Freud's couch to fall upon us and we create, through our psychoanalytic presence, new shadows for future generations of analysts.

Gallery B

Seymour Moscovitz, Ph.D.
West End Avenue
New York, New York
February 16, 2003

Barbra Locker, Ph.D.
West 81st Street
New York, New York
March 31, 2003

Gianni Nebbiosi, Ph.D.
Via Tacito
Rome, Italy
June 17, 2016

Irvin Yalom, MD
Matadero Avenue
Palo Alto, California
August 16, 2014

Liliana Pedron, Ph.D.
Avenida Federico Lacroze
Buenos Aires, Argentina
January 28, 2013

Hilary Offman, MD
Balmoral Avenue
Toronto, Canada
June 25, 2015

Beatrice Beebe, Ph.D.
West 22nd Street
New York, New York
July 31, 2015

Fabia Eleonora Banella, MA
Via Dardanelli
Rome, Italy
June 10, 2016

Liat Tsuman-Caspi, Ph.D.
Fifth Avenue
New York, New York
April 15, 2016

Bonnie Zindel, LCSW
Central Park South
New York, New York
February 9, 2015

12 Leaving the office

I have been in my current office for 12 years, the third office I have occupied for any significant time in my more than 30 years of private practice. At the start of each August break, after I have finished seeing my last patient and tidying up the loose ends on my desk, I pause at the door and look in at the room. I spend about 40 hours in this room weekly, including scheduled times for writing. My eyes survey the couch, with its colorful Mexican blanket at the bottom half of it, and the array of small pillows of varying sizes, purchased in Barcelona, that patients can rest their heads upon, or if sitting up sometimes worry the tassels at their corners. I look at the sturdy oak credenza, with its marble top, and the extended mirror above it, that houses my postcards. I sigh as I take in the bookcases containing what has evolved into my personal, professional psychoanalytic library and smile at the photographic art, images of trips to other lands.

And in this moment of pending departure, I find myself talking to the office. "I am grateful for your being a home for me and my practice. As much as I have anticipated the weeks off, away from work, I already am missing these walls that surround me." I am reminded that when Freud left Vienna, he wrote to his friend and colleague Max Eitigon: "The feeling of triumph on being liberated is too strongly mixed with sorrow, for in spite of everything I still greatly loved the prison from which I had been released" (Engelman, 1998, p. 15). As I said from the beginning, most psychoanalysts both occupy and are occupied by their offices. We take leave from the office but mostly cannot be free of our profession.

THE OFFICE AS PRISON

Allen Wheelis, the San Francisco-based writer and psychoanalyst, said:

> Only analysts have such offices. And rightly, for our profession makes us prisoners. Has it ever occurred to you, how intolerable it is to be tied in a chair? Yet we are. The rope is invisible but the immobility is our actual life. So of course we decorate our cells, import the beauty and variety of far places, of great reaches of time, to console us. It's the least we can do.
>
> (Wheelis, 1966, p. 71)

In a recent experiment, I looked over my current practice and attempted to describe my patients in categorical terms, according to what we were currently working on. I was looking for a simple account of what I do. But after a few moments, I found this line of inquiry frustrating, inadequate, and depressing. Drug dependence, marital discord, physical disability – these did not convey the powerful experience of being with an actual other, someone with a name and a personal story. Each of these people may be trapped in a cycle that repeats its origin of abandonment, boundary violations, or loss. And in the most intimate of our times together, I enter into their oppression, longing, and despondency. It is as though the patients who arrive in my office bring with them their prisons, and in spending extended time together, I, too become a prisoner. Sometimes it isn't clear who is inside the cell and who free to leave after visiting hours are over.

There was no such confusion depicted in a recent film, *Room*, based on a novel of the same name by Irish-Canadian author Emma Donoghue. Joy, a mother, and Jack, her son, are confined by Nick, Joy's abductor, rapist, father of her son, and warden of their jail room. They are guilty only of being vulnerable. In a beautiful and disturbing paper that referenced the film, Lauren Levine (2018) evoked the horrors of the vulnerable, voiceless men, women, and children trapped in solitary confinement or on death row. She described the racial inequities and intergenerational transmission of poverty and trauma that accompany these prisoners into their cells, also citing Bryan Stevenson's book, *Just Mercy* (2014). In her far-reaching analysis, she made connections among the Holocaust, rape culture, and the shame of victimhood. I choked up in reading her description of Stevenson's experience of visiting a prisoner in solitary confinement. The meeting of these two frightened human beings ended when Stevenson was forced to leave by the guards. And the prisoner, handcuffed and shackled, stood and sang a gospel song of resistance. Degradation and its transcendence were too poignantly connected for me not to cry.

In writing on mutual vulnerability, Levine (2016) provides a cautionary message that psychoanalytic work is not for the faint of heart. And make no mistake about it, contrary to the characterization of analytic rooms as being filled with the worried well, our patients find analysis when all else fails to help heal the deep wounds of cruelty imposed by other humans and by the inability to escape from the death sentence that awaits all living creatures. There is desperation at the core of every psychoanalytic treatment – if it can be seen and tolerated. And while it would be insensitive and exaggerated to equate a patient in analytic treatment with a person who is subjected to solitary confinement or a victim of a sexual predator imprisoned for years, it is still true that many of our patients are serving a life sentence of their own, imposed by past and present traumas. Providing psychoanalysis is rewarding work, and anyone fortunate enough to earn the trust of another who suffers is privileged. Yet the impact on the analyst of exposure to disturbances in and from the patient, such as disruption in regulation, assaults on developmental processes, and attacks on linking (Bion, 1959), creates a condition of secondary trauma for the analyst (Goldner, 2014). Such exposure can wear any analyst out, and by the end of a day filled with this turmoil, getting out of the office is a welcome and necessary escape.

BARTLEBY AND THE PSYCHOANALYTIC OFFICE

"Bartleby the Scrivener," perhaps the most famous short story by Herman Melville (1853), can be read as a deeply disconcerting psychoanalytic parable. It speaks to me of the damaging consequences of confinement and stands as a counterbalance to the enlightened and liberating work of the psychoanalytic office. I have endeavored in writing this book to present the office of psychoanalysis as a sacred space; yet there are times when the office must be abandoned, when the space associated with freedom of thought, emotion, and speech becomes an imprisoning hell. For me the law office in Melville's story is analogous space to such a psychoanalytic office gone bad. The title character, Bartleby, comes into the office of the narrator, a Wall Street lawyer, as a sub-clerk, and he disrupts the office over a period of time, turning it into a virtual prison, both for himself and the narrator. Ensconced in a deep cell of loss and regret is Bartleby, and he eventually imposes his imprisonment on the narrator. Similarly, there are times when a psychoanalyst is visited by a patient who will require of what seems like more than what the analyst can endure and will most likely, even with great effort on the part of the analyst, fail. The narrator in Melville's short story tries to help the unfortunate Bartleby, but in the end the lawyer must withdraw from the field.

In his first published paper in the psychoanalytic literature, Christopher Bollas (1974) compared Melville's Bartleby to the kind of patient who comes for treatment with deep character illnesses and basic faults and who induces reactions in the analyst, hoping for an opportunity for a new beginning. Every patient who comes for treatment brings an opportunity for a fresh start and, for the analyst, the prospect of learning more about psychoanalysis and about oneself. Yet embedded in the human condition, and accompanying each analysis, are the inevitable deeply held patterns and self-negating grooves which are incessantly repeated and which brought the patient into the analytic office in the first place. And the psychoanalyst also has repeating patterns, some which may resonate with the patient, since becoming an analyst is frequently an attempt at self-cure. Understanding this inescapable truth is the bane and gift of psychoanalysis. If the analysis is fortunate, it will meet this enemy of potentiality and discover that it is us!

Returning to Melville's story, we can see how the promise of a new start sometimes ends in a resounding failure. Bartleby begins well as a copyist, but one day he abruptly refuses to work, first declining to proofread and then to copy, the central task of a scrivener. He does so with the words, "I would prefer not to." This simple sentence, repeated throughout the story, contains a dignified repudiation of the cold, intractable environment of the Wall Street office of the story. And although the psychoanalytic office is the opposite of Bartleby's enclosure, with high walls on all sides and only one shaft of light, it serves a similar function as a circumscribed space, inhabited for an extended period of time, which can result in a related grounding effect.

In Bartleby's case, he makes his office his only home and refuses in both an act of defiance and liberation to carry out his required work, a deadening routine of institutional servitude. Instead, he stares out the window at a blank wall. After Bartleby takes to living in the office, the narrator becomes exasperated and tries to fire him, but he refuses to leave. The lawyer is impotent in the face of his non-violent resistance. Unable to move Bartleby, and even offering Bartleby a place in his home, which the scrivener refuses, *the lawyer himself moves out of the office*. At some point Bartleby is arrested for vagrancy and taken to jail when others complain of his refusal to leave the building. Still driven by a compassionate urge, the narrator visits Bartleby and finds he is free to roam the grassy yard but instead confines himself to studying the wall. On a subsequent visit, the lawyer observes Bartleby's huddled form lying dead at the base of a wall.

The sadness and failure of therapeutic intervention is too frequently hidden in psychoanalytic discourse. The shame associated with a collapse of the office of psychoanalysis can be a pain too great to acknowledge and must be dissoci-ated. I uncomfortably recall my work with a patient early in my career. After what seemed like a promising alliance and agreement to work in analysis five days per week, the patient abruptly became silent. No matter what I attempted (my own silence, asking questions, narrating the mood of the room), I failed to elicit any response. At some point, she moved to the swivel chair across from me and turned her back for the entirety of the session. I was locked in the imprisoning silence with my patient, who had now become my jailer. It was only in retrospect that I could begin to understand that her stance of silence was a roar of outrage for the extreme abuse she suffered as a child and the deafening silence of the adults to whose care she was entrusted. I sought out supervision, and in time she began to communicate through pages of handwritten dream notes that she gave me at the start of each session. But the silence remained. There was a thaw at some point when the memory of her abuse surfaced and she reconstructed some of the horrid violations to which she had been subject. But following a vacation break, all that had been acknowledged was now denied, and she accused me of making it all up. The silence remained like a denouncement of me as an adult and as an analyst and of analysis itself. I had hoped my therapeutic office could provide a safe place to talk, but her silence was a resounding "I would prefer not to!"

She moved away from the topic of abuse and brought in the minor annoy-ances of her life and then slowly she began to leave the treatment – reducing frequency, cancelling sessions, and stopping altogether. There is an epilogue in Melville's story, after Bartleby's death, in which the lawyer divulges a rumor about this tormented law clerk:

The report was this: that Bartleby had been a subordinate clerk in the Dead Letter Office. . . . Dead letters! Does it not sound like dead men? Sometimes from out the folded paper the pale clerk takes a ring – the finger it was meant for, perhaps, moulders in the grave; a bank-note sent in swiftest charity – he whom it would relieve, nor eats nor hungers any more; pardon for those who died unhoping; good tidings for those who died stifled by unrelieved calamities. On errands of life, these letters speed to death. Ah, Bartleby! Ah, humanity!

(Melville, 1853, p. 615)

Somewhere in my office, even though it is two iterations away from *that* room with *that* patient, lingers the failure and regret and guilt caused because I could not imagine my way into helping her, tortured by the degrading abuse and callous indifference she experienced in her life. The walls and furniture, the objects and art, cannot erase an indictment of profound inadequacy. And when this painful awareness emerges unbidden, "I need to leave the office." There are ways to get out from under the weight of the psychoanalytic office, but nonetheless, psycho-analysts always carry the office of psychoanalysis within themselves.

AN ANALYST OF MANY OFFICES

For more than 50 years, Sabert Basescu was a pillar of the New York psychoana-lytic community, particularly for those who practiced in the Interpersonal-Human-istic school. He was a beloved teacher, supervisor, and analyst, and although he did not publish extensively, was a well-regarded writer and speaker. I was greatly influenced by Sabe, as both a supervisee and patient. Before getting to know him, I heard him speak at a presentation and was dazzled by his talk on "The Anxieties in the Analyst" (Basescu, 1977). More than 30 years later, it still remains one of my favorite psychoanalytic papers. In a tribute to Sabe's work, Irwin Hoffman (2010) noted, "everything Sabe is teaching us . . . is simply that the therapist or analyst is a person, a human being, and that the analytic role, however it affects the nature of the analyst's involvement, does not negate that simple reality" (p. 30).

Sabe's integrity was a reliable ballast during the sometimes bumpy journey of my analysis with him and also in the supervision that preceded that. What was striking about my visits to Sabe's office was that the physical space changed often, but Sabe's essential presence did not. I saw him over an 18-year period (intermit-tently, in three analytic segments and a year of supervision) and in six different offices. There was the small windowless room that was in the analytic institute in which I was in training, the borrowed office of another analyst, a few rather non-descript rooms in older Manhattan residential buildings, and even an office in his suburban home, that in my recollection had the feel of a slightly stuffy basement recreation room. Sabe did not seem to put much emphasis on the environment in which analysis took place. I have a memory that he told me once he conducted sessions while lying on the floor of his office, because of back pain, and that he met with patients in his car at another time. I never got to discuss these matters with him and wish that I could have. His near-fatal bike collision in 2006, from which he never made a full recovery, stopped our work together and preceded my own more developed ideas about the psychoanalytic office. He died in 2018.

During a period of terminating one of the segments of analysis, I asked if I could photograph him. After a number of sessions discussing the meaning and feelings around my request, he agreed, and the photo I took and printed became a parting gift. This photograph was an important step on my road to creating the project that now includes so many portraits of psychoanalysts in their offices. His many offices and his steady presence hover over my own psychoanalytic space.

MASHA BOROVIKOVA, A PRINCIPLED SPIRIT

While for some analysts, such as Sabe Basescu, the physical space in which they work may be somewhat incidental, for new analysts, borrowing space puts additional pressure on them to create their own environment in which they can nurture both themselves and their patients within someone else's office. When I asked to photograph Masha Borovikova, she had recently completed her internship and doctoral program in clinical psychology and was in psychoanalytic training. She said, "I have no office of my own, but am mooching off a friend of a friend who is letting me occupy her space when it is not in use." She added, "Here is sincerely hoping this is NOT the future of psychoanalysis!" Regarding the design of the office, Masha wrote,

> I am subletting the space part-time, so nothing in it is of me, so to speak. I try to disturb the space as little as possible with my presence – leave no trace behind. The decorations/design are minimal; they do not particularly reflect my taste, but don't offend my sensibilities either.
>
> (personal communication, July 28, 2018)

Although the office was not designed or furnished by her, her distinctive presence while there made it her own space.

Masha immigrated from Russia to the United States when she was 17. She studied acting and psychology as an undergraduate and then completed an MFA in acting before getting her doctorate in psychology. Masha said she felt uncomfortable in front of a camera under everyday circumstances, unlike how she felt when she had done stage and TV work. This was not obvious to me during the photoshoot, in which Masha occupied her place and created a powerful statement. I realized later, when I looked at the images on the computer, that the statement of this relational image was one of "a principled spirit." She told me a moving story from her childhood which reflected what had come through in her photograph. In Russia all 16-year-olds had to apply for a passport. Children looked forward to this momentous occasion, perhaps in the same way that American children look forward to getting a driver's license. The application required listing parents' ethnicities as well as the adolescent's declared ethnicity. Masha's father was an ethnic Slav, and her mother was Jewish. In the patrilineal Russian system, children typically take the ethnicity of their fathers, but Masha had promised her Jewish friend she would not turn away from that part of her heritage. This promise

Masha Borovikova, Ph.D.
West 58th Street
New York, New York
July 28, 2018

occurred when they were both six and looking forward to their 16th birthday. Her friend's parents were both Jewish, and she said to Masha, "I know when you get your passport you will identify yourself as Russian." Masha responded that she would declare herself Jewish, in solidarity, and a decade later she kept that promise, although she and her childhood friend were no longer in contact. This powerful and unusual action, which carried repercussions for state sponsored anti-Semitic quotas and sanctions, was exceptional for such a young person. She was required to sign an affidavit declaring that she identified herself as Jewish of her own free will. Her stance was especially noteworthy because her family did not practice Judaism, consciously stopping in her grandparents' generation under Stalinist rule.

The position of taking a stand may have been influenced by her father's spirited independence. In response to a question about the effect of her childhood home on her sense of comfort, she told me about her father:

> My childhood apartment (in St. Petersburg, Russia) was renovated under my Dad's guidance when I was five or six. He hand-picked this fantastical wallpaper with bright-colored flowering vines running vertically up and down the wall. It's still a mystery to me where and how he was able to procure such a jarringly un-Soviet thing (bribery was involved, no doubt). He decided to wallpaper the ceilings also, which was very unusual, at least for that time and place – most apartments you would visit looked drab back then, just the way you would imagine them. After that my room looked and felt like a whimsical, cozy toy box. Come to think of it now, years later, in graduate school, I wrote a solo performance piece about waking up in a shoe box, over and over again. I suppose I take comfort in boxes, but not feeling boxed in, something like that?
>
> (personal communication, July 26, 2018)

Masha Borovikova is an example of how new voices keep the psychoanalytic field continuously vital. The infusion of Masha and many in her cohort bring greater diversity and challenge to deeply held assumptions and patterns that have accompanied psychoanalysis from its origins in nineteenth-century Central Europe. As a refugee and a woman in a world where fascistic, racist, and misogynistic policies and attitudes are reemerging, people like Masha are adding new insights and the benefit of their own experiences. I was impressed by this passage, appearing on her *Psychology Today* page:

> I have commanded foreign words to explicate the native in me, all the while obfuscating what was, but was not, could not be, spoken. And what of words? I have spoken in multitudes and platitudes. I have harbored thoughts and feelings with no hope of setting them off to sail in these words. All words but my own. There are, and always will be, two ways to tell my stories. I shall strive to choose dis-cordingly. There once was word where my innards stood. First there was word. After word there was silence.

This introduction is followed by a description of the kinds of problems she works with (including survivor trauma, psychosis, and immigration) and ends with the statement, "I will work in English, Russian, and silence." Silence was a theme during the discussion we shared in the photoshoot. There wasn't that much of it during our conversation, except for some quiet moments that might allow reverie and respect. But there was another silence brought up in response to a dangerous and despotic world, one where the specter of being sexually attacked on the street during adolescence was a constant companion and one in which the menace of being marched off to death and separated from her maternal connection without the power of words were nightmarish realities. For psychoanalysis to survive, voices such as Masha's cannot be silenced.

TAKING A BREAK

Over time all kinds of human experience are brought into a psychoanalytic office, including happy moments and fortunate times, problem solving around mutually desirable options, and profound appreciation for basic health and simple pleasures. Yet the theme of loss is part of the lives of patients: their suffering from trauma, neglect, and despair, which they bring with hope for relief from constant and vigilant dread, unwanted self-attacking thoughts, and painful feelings of helplessness. Sometimes all our training and experience and devotion to the work cannot penetrate the emotional power of loss, which enters the office and will not leave, like the raven in Poe's famous poem. When the world seems cold and mean and there is so much pain and rage in people's lives, analysts, like all people, are vulnerable to sorrow. We seek surcease in books, family and friends, vacations, and distractions of all kinds but can find ourselves, like the poet, unable to get out from under that shadow of grief. Thus we must find ways to heal ourselves, and getting out of the office can be an important therapeutic act.

A cover story in the Travel section of *The New York Times*, titled, "Finding Yourself in Los Angeles," described some special places in the city that were escapes from the stress of life in La La Land. One was the house of the legendary modernist designers, Charles and Ray Eames. The author said:

> And it is this duality that I am drawn to: that a private space of contemplation can also be a place of intense activation. A retreat is not so much a retreat but a re-turn, a re-think, a re-view, in its literal sense. All my best ideas have come when I have stepped away from my office, when I am in the shower or running or shinrin-yoku-ing and have a chance to view my work from a new angle.
>
> (Larsen, 2018)

Writing is another means to view my work from a new angle. Having the opportunity to write about the psychoanalytic office and read so many articles, books, and stories about psychoanalysis, photography, architecture and design, and myriad other subjects has provided another perspective by which to see and experience

Spyros Orfanos, Ph.D.
2nd Avenue
New York, New York
December 13, 2003

my work. This outlet shores up the openness and strength necessary to honor my patients in their struggles. My dear colleague, Spyros Orfanos, whom I photographed in 2003, has likened the work of psychoanalysts to that of professional mourners (Orfanos, 2014).

As a young boy I made many visits to the cemetery with my family. Two grandparents died before I was ten, and a number of my mother's older siblings were buried in United Hebrew Cemetery on Staten Island. There were other occasions, in addition to funerals, for visiting the cemetery: Yahzeits, the anniversary of a loved one's death; Mother's or Father's Day; and before Rosh Hashanah, the Jewish New Year. Rather than feeling spooked, I was fascinated by the cemetery. It was often a time the extended family got together, and I would see many of my New Jersey cousins as we converged from our different land masses onto Staten Island. But of most interest to me were the old men roaming the cemetery grounds. They were dressed in black, had beards and peyos (curled sidelocks worn by Orthodox Jewish men), carried tattered prayer books, and would approach grieving families with an offer to say prayers. In exchange for their davening lamentations (prayers during which they rocked back and forth), they would be given some money. Although some in my family saw this as a degrading form of begging and rejected the "schnorrer's" (beggar's) act, I was taken by these professional mourners. Paid mourners exist in many cultures. In many instances they have been women, and one scholar makes a case that that wailing women in the Bible carried on a professional trade that required training (Claassens, 2012). Are we psychoanalysts the new professional mourners?

I am writing these words on a Sunday afternoon in October. It's an unusually warm day, although the grey sky tells more of the coming of fall than the passage of summer. One of the places my reading took me during the writing of this book was to Daniel Mendelsohn's *An Odyssey*, a poignant story of a search for home and for a father. I feel very connected to these themes. Mendelsohn's memoir is both a retelling of Homer's *Odyssey* and the story of a complicated father–son relationship. He described the origin of the word "nostalgia," a combination of the Greek words, *nostos*, an epic tale of homecoming, with *algos* which means pain, so nostalgia is "the pain associated with longing for home" (2017, p. 93). I relate very much to this yearning. Even before the first psychoanalytic home was destroyed by the Nazis in Vienna, it had been a place of mourning for Freud, a mausoleum of tribute to death (Fuss & Sanders, 2004). My dream of an office began in my father's workplace and contained the shadow of his death. Such shadows of bereavement are deeply etched into the walls of all psychoanalytic offices. With the help of our cherished profession, we mourn our losses and celebrate life.

Each August as I prepare to leave for summer break and lock the door, after checking that the vacation message is clear on my answering machine, I feel the intense sense of freedom I still remember from my childhood days of the end of the school year. Being released is exhilarating, but shortly after, some anxiety creeps in. Will my patients be okay without me? Will I without them? "It will all be fine," I tell myself, because I'll be returning in September. I'll be back in the chair. Most patients will return. I comfort myself, momentarily ignoring the reality that time is passing. Being free only has meaning in its relationship to being restricted. And despite the depths and heights of psychoanalytic travel that we, with our patients, undertake in our offices, we inhabit a confined space that is necessary and desirable. It is our treasured home and our lonely prison.

References

Abramovitch, H. (1997). Temenos lost: Reflections on moving. *Journal of Analytic Psychology, 42*(4), 569–584.

Abramovitch, H. (2002). Temenos regained: Reflections on the absence of the analyst. *Journal of Analytic Psychology, 47*(4), 583–598.

Akhtar, S. (2009). *The damaged core: Origins, dynamics, manifestations, and treatment.* Lanham, MD: Jason Aronson.

Aran, S. (2017, June 14). Gaston Bachelard: Home is where the heart is. *Bonjour Paris.* Retrieved from https://bonjourparis.com/history/philosopher-gaston-bachelard/

Aron, L., & Atlas, G. (2015). Generative enactment: Memories from the future. *Psychoanalytic Dialogues, 25,* 309–324. doi:10.1080/10481885.2015.1034554

Atwood, G. (2015). Credo and reflections. *Psychoanalytic Dialogues, 25*(2), 137–152.

Atwood, M. (1995). *Morning in the burned house.* New York, NY: Houghton Mifflin Harcourt Publishing.

Auden, W. H. (1939). In memory of Sigmund Freud. In *Another time.* New York, NY: Random House.

Bachelard, G. (1958/1994). *The poetics of space: The classic look at how we experience intimate places.* Boston, MA: Beacon Press.

Balint, M. (1954). Analytic training and training analysis. *International Journal of Psychoanalysis, 35,* 157–162.

Barthes, R. (1981). *Camera Lucida: Reflections on photography.* New York, NY: Hill & Wang.

Basescu, S. (1977). Anxieties in the analyst: An autobiographical account. In K. A. Frank (Ed.), *The human dimension in psychoanalytic practice* (pp. 153–163). New York, NY: Grune & Stratton.

Bass, A. (2007). When the frame doesn't fit the picture. *Psychoanalytic Dialogues, 17*(1), 1–27.

Bass, A. (2015). The dialogue of unconsciousness, mutual analysis and the uses of the self in contemporary relational psychoanalysis. *Psychoanalytic Dialogues, 25*(1), 2–17.

Becker, E. (1973). *The denial of death.* New York, NY: Simon & Schuster.

Beckett, S. (1958). *The unnamable.* New York, NY: Grove Press.

Beebe, B., Cohen, P., & Lachmann, F. (2016). *The mother-infant interaction picture book: Origins of attachment.* New York, NY: W. W. Norton & Company.

Beebe, B., Rustin, J., Sorter, D., & Knoblauch, S. (2003). An expanded view of intersubjectivity in infancy and its application to psychoanalysis. *Psychoanalytic Dialogues, 19*(5), 805–841.

Bell, K. (2013). *The artist's house: From workplace to artwork.* Berlin: Sternberg Press.

Benjamin, J. (1988). *The bonds of love: Psychoanalysis, feminism, and the problem of domination.* New York, NY: Pantheon.

Benjamin, J. (1990). An outline of intersubjectivity: The development of recognition. *Psychoanalytic Psychology, 7,* 33–46. doi:10.1037/h0085258

■ References

Benjamin, J. (2004). Beyond doer and done to. *Psychoanalytic Quarterly*, *73*(1), 5–46.

Benjamin, W. (1933). Experience and poverty. In R. Livingstone (Trans.), *Die Welt im Wort*, *Gesammelte Schriften* (Vol. II, pp. 213–219). Retrieved from http://atlasofplaces.com/Experience-and-Poverty-Walter-Benjamin

Benvenuto, S. (1995–1996). Interview with Andre Green: Against Lacanism. *European Journal of Psychoanalysis*, *2*. Retrieved from www.journal-psychoanalysis.eu/against-lacanism-a-conversation-with-andre-green/

Bergmann, M. S. (1993). Psychoanalytic education and the social reality of psychoanalysis. *Psychoanalytic Review*, *80*(2), 199–210.

Bernstein, J. W. (2000). Making a memorial place: The photography of Shimon Attie. *Psychoanalytic Dialogues*, *10*, 347–370.

Bion, W. R. (1959). Attacks on linking. *International Journal of Psycho-Analysis*, *40*, 308–315.

Bion, W. R. (1967/2013). Notes on memory and desire. In J. Aguayo & B. Malin (Eds), *Wilfred Bion: Los Angeles seminars and supervision* (pp. 136–138). London: Karnac Books.

Blechner, M. (2001). *The dream frontier*. New York, NY: Routledge.

Bollas, C. (1974). Melville's lost self: Bartleby. *American Imago*, *31*(4), 401–411.

Bollas, C. (1987). *The shadow of the object: Psychoanalysis of the unthought known*. London: Free Association Books.

Bollas, C. (1989). *Forces of destiny: Psychoanalysis and human idiom*. Oxford: Free Association Books.

Brenner, F. (2003). *Diaspora*. Exhibit at Brooklyn Museum of Art.

Burka, J. (2001). The therapist's body in reality and fantasy: A perspective from an overweight therapist. In B. Gerson (Ed.), *The therapist as a person*. New York, NY: Routledge.

Cardinal, M. (1983). *The words to say it*. Cambridge, MA: VanVactor & Goodheart.

Civitarese, G. (2014). Between "other" and "other": Merleau-Ponty as a precursor of the analytic field. *Fort Da*, *20*(1), 9–29.

Cixous, H. (1993). *Three steps on the ladder of writing*. New York, NY: Columbia University Press.

Claassens, L. J. M. (2012). *Mourner, mother, midwife: Reimagining God's delivering presence in the old testament*. Louisville, KY: Westminster John Knox Press.

Clemens, N. A. (2011). A psychiatrist retires: An oxymoron? *Journal of Psychiatric Practice*, *17*(5), 351–354.

Cole, T. (2015, October 14). On photography: Memories of things unseen. *The New York Times Magazine*. Retrieved from www.nytimes.com/2015/10/18/magazine/memories-of-things-unseen.html

Colson, D. (1979). Photography as an extension of the ego. *International Review of Psychoanalysis*, *6*, 273–282.

Corpt, E. A. (2013). Peasant in the analyst's chair: Reflections, personal and otherwise, on class and the forming of an analytic identity. *International Journal of Psychoanalytic Self Psychology*, *8*(1), 52–69.

Cosgrove, B. (2014/1933). *Behind the picture: Joseph Goebbels Glares at the camera*. Geneva. Retrieved from time.com/3880669/goebbels-in-geneva-1933-behind-a-classic-alfred-eisenstaedt-photo/

Danze, E. A. (2005). An architect's view of introspective space: The analytic vessel. *Annual of Psychoanalysis*, *33*, 109–124.

Davidson, J. (2017). *Magnetic city: A walking companion to New York*. New York, NY: Spiegel & Grau.

Delistraty, C. (2017, July 13). *The revolutionary virtue of life in a glass house*. Retrieved from https://delistraty.com/2017/07/13/the-revolutionary-virtue-of-life-in-a-glass-house/

Dillon, B. (2011, March 25). Rereading: Camera Lucida by Roland Barthes. *The Guardian*. Retrieved from www.theguardian.com/books/2011/mar/26/roland-barthes-camera-lucida-rereading

Dimen, M. (2011). *Lapsus linguae*, or a slip of the tongue? A sexual violation in an analytic treatment and its personal and theoretical aftermath. *Contemporary Psychoanalysis*, *47*(1), 35–79.

Domash, L. (2014). Creating therapeutic "space": How architecture and design can inform psychoanalysis. *Psychoanalytic Perspectives*, *11*(2), 94–111.

Doolittle, H. (1974). *Tribute to Freud*. New York, NY: New Directions.

Dosamantes-Beaudry, I. (1997). Somatic experience in psychoanalysis. *Psychoanalytic Psychology*, *14*, 517–530.

Dyer, G. (2017, January 18). On photography: The mysteries of our family snapshots. *The New York Times*. Retrieved from www.nytimes.com/2017/01/03/magazine/the-mysteries-of-our-family-snapshots.html

Edwards, A., & Polite, C. K. (1992). *Children of the dream: The psychology of black success*. Norwell, MA: Anchor Press.

Ekstein, R. (1979/1977). Review of "My analysis with Freud: Reminiscences: by A. Kardiner M.D." *Psychoanalytic Quarterly*, *48*(31), 123.

Eliot, T. S. (1944). East Coker. In T. S. Eliot, *Four quartets*. London: Faber & Faber.

Engelman, E. (1976). *Bergasse 19: Sigmund Freud's home and offices, Vienna 1938*. New York, NY: Basic Books.

Engelman, E. (1998). *Bergasse 19: Sigmund Freud's home and offices, Vienna, 1938*. New York, NY: Basic Books.

Falzeder, E. (2005). Psychoanalytic filiations. *Cabinet Magazine*.

Falzeder, E. (2015). *Psychoanalytic filiations: Mapping the psychoanalytic movement*. London: Karnac Books.

Ferro, A. (2008). A beam of intense darkness. *International Journal of Psychoanalysis*, *89*(4), 867–884.

Foucault, M. (1964/1988). *Madness and civilization*. New York, NY: Vintage.

Frankiel, R. (Ed.). (1994). *Essential papers on object loss*. New York, NY: New York University Press.

Freud, A. (1951). August Aichhorn, July 27, 1878 – October 17, 1949. *International Journal of Psycho-Analysis*, *32*, 51–56.

Freud, S. (1905/1963). *Dora: An analysis of a case of hysteria*. New York, NY: Palgrave Macmillan.

Freud, S. (1912). Recommendations to physicians practising psycho-analysis. In J. Strachey (Ed. & Trans. 1958), *The standard edition of the complete psychological works of Sigmund Freud, Volume XII (1911–1913): The case of Schreber, papers on technique and other works* (pp. 109–120). London: Hogarth Press.

Freud, S. (1913). On beginning the treatment (further recommendations on the technique of psycho-analysis). In J. Strachey (Ed. & Trans. 1958), *The standard edition of the complete psychological works of Sigmund Freud, Volume XII (1911–1913): The case of Schreber, papers on technique and other work* (pp. 121–144). London: Hogarth Press.

Freud, S. (1917). Introductory lectures on psycho-analysis. In J. Strachey (Ed. & Trans. 1963), *The standard edition of the complete psychological works of Sigmund Freud, Volume XVI (1916–1917): Introductory lectures on psycho-analysis (part III)* (pp. 241–463). London: Hogarth Press.

Freud, S. (1930). Civilization and its discontents. In J. Strachey (Ed. & Trans.1961), *The standard edition of the complete psychological works of Sigmund Freud, Volume XXI (1927–1931): The future of an illusion, civilization and its discontents, and other works* (pp. 57–146). London: Hogarth Press.

Freud, S. (1931). Letter to the Burgomaster of Příbor. In J. Strachey (Ed. & Trans. 1961), *The standard edition of the complete psychological works of Sigmund Freud, Volume XXI (1927–1931): The future of an illusion, civilization and its discontents, and other works* (pp. 259–260) London: Hogarth Press.

Freud, S. (1937). Analysis terminable and interminable. In J. Strachey (Ed. & Trans.1964), *The standard edition of the complete psychological works of Sigmund Freud, Volume XXIII*

■ References

(1937–1939): Moses and monotheism, an outline of psycho-analysis and other works (pp. 209–254). London: Hogarth Press.

Freud, S. (1940/1949). *An outline of psychoanalysis.* New York, NY: W. W. Norton & Company.

Fromm, M. G. (1989). Photography as transitional functioning. In G. Fromm & B. Smith (Eds), *The facilitating environment: Clinical applications of Winnicott's theories.* Madison, CT: International Universities Press.

Frost, R. (1913). *A boy's will.* New York, NY: Henry Holt and Company.

Fuss, D. (2004). *The sense of an interior: Four writers and the rooms that shaped them.* New York, NY: Routledge.

Fuss, D., & Sanders, J. (2004). Freud's ear: Bergasse 19 Vienna Austria. In D. Fuss (Ed.), *The sense of an interior: Four writers and the rooms that shaped them.* New York, NY: Routledge.

Gargiulo, G. J. (2007). Framing the question: Psychoanalytic process, the unconscious, and home offices – an alternate perspective. *Psychoanalytic Psychology, 24*(4), 715–719.

Gay, P. (1988). *Freud: A life for our time.* New York, NY: W. W. Norton & Company.

Gerald, M. (2011). The psychoanalytic office: Past, present, and future. *Psychoanalytic Psychology, 28*(3), 435–445. doi:10.1037/a0024209

Gerald, M. (2013, April 13). *You can take the boy out of the Bronx.* Paper presented at Program Architecture as Potential Space: Reflections and a Roundtable Conversation. New York University Postdoctoral in Psychoanalysis and Psychotherapy, New York, NY.

Gerald, M. (2014). The stain on the rug: Commentary on paper by Leanne Domash. *Psychoanalytic Perspectives, 11*, 112–121.

Gerald, M. (2015). Psychoanalytic lens of Mark Gerald: In the shadow of Freud's couch. *GDC Interiors Journal.* Retrieved from www.gdcinteriors.com/psychoanalytic-space-by-design/

Gerald, M. (2016). The cracks are where the light comes in. *Psychoanalytic Dialogues, 26*(5), 592–598.

Goldberg, V. (1986, September). Alfred Eisenstaedt finally gets his first full retrospective. *New York Magazine, 9*(36), 80.

Goldner, V. (2014). Attachment, recognition, and secondary trauma: Reply to commentaries. *Psychoanalytic Dialogues, 24*(4), 433–440.

Goodyear, S. (2015, March 3). A new campaign takes aim at New York's growing chain stores. *The Atlantic.* City Lab. Retrieved from www.citylab.com/equity/2015/03/a-new-campaign-takes-aim-at-new-yorks-growing-chain-stores/386695/

Gopnik, A. (1998, August 24, 31). Annals of psychoanalysis: Man goes to see a doctor. *The New Yorker.* Retrieved from www.newyorker.com/magazine/1998/08/24/man-goes-to-see-a-doctor

Goren, E. (2003). America's love affair with technology: The transformation of sexuality and the self over the 20th century. *Psychoanalytic Psychology, 20*(3), 487–508.

Gorlin, A. (2013, April). Paper presented at Architecture as Potential Space: Reflections and a Roundtable Conversation. New York University Postdoctoral Program in Psychoanalysis, New York, NY.

Green, A. (1986/2005). The dead mother. In A. Green (Ed.), *On private madness* (pp. 142–173). London: Karnac.

Greenberg, J., & Mitchell, S. (1983). *Object relations in psychoanalytic theory.* Boston, MA: Harvard University Press.

Greenspan, E. (2013, August 28). Daniel Libeskind's world trade center change of heart. *The New Yorker.* Retrieved from www.newyorker.com/business/currency/daniel-libeskinds-world-trade-center-change-of-heart

Grinker, R. R., Jr. (2001). My father's analysis with Sigmund Freud. *Annual Review of Psychoanalysis, 29*, 35–47.

Grosskurth, P. (1986). *Melanie Klein: Her world and her work.* New York, NY: Knopf.

Grotjahn, M. (1973/1971). Diary of my analysis with Sigmund Freud: By Smiley Blanton M.D. *Psychoanalytic Quarterly, 42*, 272–274. New York, NY: Hawthorn Books, Inc, p. 141.

Grotstein, J. S. (2008). *A beam of darkness*. London: Karnac Books.

Hamilton, J. W. (1995). To see the thing itself: The influence of early object loss on the life and art of Edward Weston. *Journal of the American Academy of Psychoanalysis, 23*, 671–691.

Harris, A. (2000). Gender as a soft assembly: Tomboys' stories. *Studies in Gender and Sexuality, 1*(3), 223–250.

Harris, M. E. (2000). Arnold Newman: The stories behind some of the most famous portraits in the 20th century. *American Photo, 11*(2), 36–38.

Henkel, L. A. (2014). Point-and-shoot memories: The influence of taking photos on memory for a museum tour. *Psychological Science, 25*(2), 396–402.

Hershberg, S. (2016). *Changing the physical aspects of the analytic setting: The impact on the analyst, the patient and the relationship and its home*. Unpublished paper.

Hespos, S. J., & Spelke, E. S. (2004). Conceptual precursors to language. *Nature, 430*(6998), 453–456.

Hoffman, I. (2010). Anxieties in the analyst: Commentary. In G. Goldstein & H. Golden (Eds), *Sabert Basescu: Selected papers on human nature and psychoanalysis* (pp. 29–36). New York, NY: Routledge.

Holliss, F. (2012). *The workhome . . . A new building type?* London: London Metropolitan University.

Hyman, I. (2013, December 30). Photographs and memories. *Psychology Today*. Retrieved from www.psychologytoday.com/us/blog/mental-mishaps/201312/photographs-and-memories

Jacobs, T. (1991). *The use of the self. Countertransference and communication in the analytic situation*. New York, NY: International Universities Press.

Johnson, R. (2014). Kant's moral philosophy. In *The Stanford encyclopedia of philosophy* (Summer 2014 edition). Retrieved from https://plato.stanford.edu/archives/sum2014/entries/kant-moral/

Kilborne, B. (2002). *Disappearing persons: Shame and appearance*. Albany, NY: SUNY Press.

Knoblauch, S. H. (2007). The perversion of language in the analyst's activity: Navigating the rhythms of embodiment and symbolization. *International Forum of Psychoanalysis, 16*(1), 38–42.

Kohon, G. (Ed.). (1999). *The dead mother: The work of Andre Green*. London: Routledge.

Kravis, N. (2017). *On the couch: A repressed history of the analytic couch from Plato to Freud*. Boston, MA: The MIT Press.

Kuchuck, S. (2014). *Clinical implications of the psychoanalyst's life experience: When the personal becomes professional*. New York, NY: Routledge.

Kuhn, T. (1962). *The structure of scientific revolutions*. Chicago, IL: The University of Chicago Press.

Lacan, J. (1964/1978). The split between the eye and the gaze. In A. Sheridan (Trans.), *The four fundamental concepts of psychoanalysis* (pp. 67–78). New York, NY: W. W. Norton & Company.

Langs, R. (2007). One mind or two: Divergent views of the home-office setting. *Psychoanalytic Psychology, 24*(1), 180–186.

Larsen, R. (2018, July 23). Finding yourself in Los Angeles. *The New York Times*. Retrieved from www.nytimes.com/2018/07/23/travel/los-angeles-retreats-spiritual.html

Leffert, M. (2003). Analysis and psychotherapy by telephone: Twenty years of clinical experience. *Journal of American Psychoanalytic Association, 51*, 101–130.

Lefort, C. (1968). *The visible and the invisible: Maurice Merleau-Ponty*. Evanston, IL: Northwestern University Press.

Levenson, E. A. (1972). *The fallacy of understanding: An inquiry into the changing structure of psychoanalysis*. New York, NY: Basic Books.

Levenson, E. A. (1983). *The ambiguity of change*. Northvale, NJ: Jason Aronson.

Levenson, E. A. (2003). On seeing what is said: Visual aides to the psychoanalytic process. *Contemporary Psychoanalysis, 39*(2), 233–249.

■ References

Levine, L. (2016). Mutual vulnerability: Intimacy, psychic collisions, and the shards of trauma. *Psychoanalytic Dialogues, 26*(5), 571–579.

Levine, L. (2018, June). *Creative means of staying enlivened when locked in an endless present.* Paper presented at the IARPP 16th Annual Conference on Hope and Dread: Therapists and Patients in an Uncertain World, New York, NY.

Libeskind, D. (2012). *Architecture is a language.* Retrieved from https://libeskind.com/publishing/tedx/

Lippmann, P. (2011, April). *On the nature of disappearance: A modern existential dilemma.* Paper presented at the 31st Annual Spring Meeting of the American Psychological Association, Division of Psychoanalysis (39), New York, NY.

Lipton, L. (2001). Long distance psychoanalysis. *Clinical Social Work Journal, 29*(1), 35–52.

Liss-Levinson, N. (1990). Money matters and the woman analyst: In a different voice. *Psychoanalytic Psychology, 7S*(Supplement), 119–130.

Loewenberg, P. (2004). Lucian and Sigmund Freud. *American Imago, 61*(1), 89–99.

Mahler, M., Pine, F., & Bergman, A. (2000). *The psychological birth of the human infant: Symbiosis and individuation.* New York, NY: Basic Books.

Malcolm, J. (1982). *Psychoanalysis: The impossible profession.* New York, NY: Vintage.

Maroda, K. J. (2007). Ethical considerations of the home office. *Psychoanalytic Psychology, 24*(1), 173–179.

McDougall, J. (1989). *Theatres of the body.* New York, NY: W. W. Norton & Company.

McDougall, J. (1992). *Plea for a measure of abnormality.* New York, NY: Brunner, Mazel.

McLaughlin, J. T. (1995). Touching limits in the analytic dyad. *Psychoanalytic Quarterly, 64,* 433–465.

Melville, H. (1853). *Bartleby, the Scrivener: A story of wall-street* [as contained in *Putnam's monthly magazine of American literature, science, and art,* Vol. II. July–December 1853].

Mendelsohn, D. (2017). *An Odyssey: A father, a son, and an epic.* New York, NY: Knopf.

Merleau-Ponty, M. (1968). *The visible and the invisible.* Evanston, IL: Northwestern University Press.

Mills, J. (2007). The immorality of the home office. *Psychoanalytic Psychology, 24*(4), 720–723.

Mitchell, S. A. (1998). The emergence of features of the analyst's life. *Psychoanalytic Dialogues, 8*(2), 187–194.

Molino, A. (1997). *Freely associated: Encounters in psychoanalysis with Christopher Bollas, Joyce McDougall, Michael Eigen, Adam Phillips and Nina Coltart.* London: Free Association Books.

Morris, E. (2011). *Believing is seeing (Observations on the mysteries of photography).* New York, NY: Penguin Press.

Moser, M. (2017, June 30). *Margaret Moser tribute: Lucinda Williams, the life of the party.* Retrieved from www.austinchronicle.com/music/2017-06-30/margaret-moser-tribute-lucinda-williams-lucinda-williams/

Moss, J. (2017). *Vanishing New York: How a great city lost its soul.* New York, NY: Harper Collins.

Moss, J. (2018, March 7). The death and life of a great American building. *The New York Review of Books.* Retrieved from www.nybooks.com/daily/2018/03/07/the-death-and-life-of-a-great-american-building/

Mulvey, L. (1999). *Visual and other pleasures* (2nd edn). New York, NY: Palgrave Macmillan.

Nass, M. L. (2015). The omnipotence of the psychoanalyst: Thoughts on the need to consider retirement. *Journal of the American Psychoanalytic Association, 63*(5), 1013–1023.

Newman, A. (2000). *Arnold Newman.* Kohn, Germany: Taschen.

Ogden, T. H. (1994). The analytic third: Working with intersubjective clinical facts. *International Journal of Psycho-Analysis, 75,* 3–19.

Ogden, T. H. (2000). Borges and the art of mourning. *Psychoanalytic Dialogues, 10,* 65–88.

Ogden, T. H. (2003). On not being able to dream. *International Journal of Psycho-Analysis*, *84*(1), 17–30.

Orfanos, S. D. (2014). An epiphany on the Acropolis. *Contemporary Psychoanalysis*, *50*(4), 659–680.

Ornstein, A. (2010). The missing tombstone: Reflections on mourning and creativity. *Journal of the American Psychoanalytic Association*, *58*, 631–648.

Orwell, G. (1950/1977). *1984*. New York, NY: Penguin.

Osgood, C. (2013, May 19). The psychology of design and color. *CBS Sunday Morning*. Retrieved from www.cbsnews.com/videos/the-psychology-of-design-and-color

Parsons, K. C. (Ed.). (1998). *The writings of Clarence Stein: Architect of the planned community*. Baltimore, MD: Johns Hopkins University Press.

Peltz, R. (2012, May). *A new thing has been created – A discussion of resonances and reverberations*. Discussion of Surface, Space and Artifact: The Material Presence of Memory – Julie Levitt's Graduation Paper. Psychoanalytic Institute of Northern California, San Francisco, CA.

Peltz, R. (2014). Our bodies, ourselves, others, and the world: An introduction to Merleau-Ponty's philosophy of inter-corporeality. *Fort Da*, *20*(1), 30–32.

Rappoport, E. (2012). Creating the umbilical cord: Relational knowing and the somatic third. *Psychoanalytic Dialogues*, *22*(3), 375–388.

Razinsky, L. (2014). *Freud, psychoanalysis, and death*. New York, NY: Cambridge University Press.

Richman, S. (2013). Out of darkness: Reverberations of trauma and its creative transformations. *Psychoanalytic Dialogues*, *23*(3), 362–376. doi:10.1080/10481885.2013.794647

Ringstrom, P. A. (2007). Scenes that write themselves: Improvisational moments in relational psychoanalysis. *Psychoanalytic Dialogues*, *17*(1), 69–99.

Roiphe, K. (2016). *The violet hour: Great writers at the end*. New York, NY: The Dial Press.

Roth, D. (2006). Adornment as a method of interior design. *Studies in Gender and Sexuality*, *7*(2), 179–194.

Sartre, J. (1964). *Being and nothingness* (H. E. Barnes, trans.). New York, NY: Citadel Press.

Scharff, J. S. (2012). Clinical issues in analysis over the telephone and the Internet. *International Journal of Psycho-Analysis*, *93*(1), 81–95.

Schepeler, E. M. (1993). Jean Piaget's experiences on the couch: Some clues to a mystery. *International Journal of Psycho-Analysis*, *74*, 255–273.

Schilling, J. (2013, May 25). Lucinda Williams interview: I've earned the right to say what I like. *The Telegraph*. Retrieved from www.telegraph.co.uk/culture/music/worldfol kandjazz/10074160/Lucinda-Williams-interview-Ive-earned-the-right-to-say-what-I-like.html

Sebald, W. G. (2001). *Austerlitz* (A. Bell, trans.). New York, NY: Random House.

Seiden, H. M. (2009). On the longing for home. *Psychoanalytic Psychology*, *26*(2), 191–205.

Shams, L., & Seitz, A. R. (2008). Benefits of multi sensory learning. *Trends in Cognitive Sciences*, *12*(11), 411–417.

Singer, E. (1977/2017). The fiction of analytic anonymity. In D. B. Stern & I. Hirsch (Eds), *The interpersonal perspective in psychoanalysis, 1960s–1990s*. New York, NY: Routledge.

Singer, M. (2015). Unbroken chain. *Psychoanalytic Perspectives*, *12*(1), 101–102.

Smith, H. F. (2001). Hearing voices: The fate of the analyst's identifications. *Journal of the American Psychoanalytic Association*, *49*(3), 781–812.

Sontag, S. (1973). *On photography*. New York, NY: Farrar, Straus, Giroux.

Sperber, E. (2014). Sublimation: Building or dwelling? Loewald, Freud, and architecture. *Psychoanalytic Psychology*, *31*(4), 507–524.

Sperber, E. (2016). The wings of Daedalus: Toward a relational architecture. *Psychoanalytic Review*, *103*(5), 593–617.

■ References

Stack, C. (1999). Psychoanalysis meets queer theory: An encounter with the terrifying other. *Gender and Psychoanalysis, 4*(1), 71–87.

Stevenson, B. (2014). *Just mercy: A story of justice and redemption.* New York, NY: Spiegel & Grau.

Stewart, S. (1986). *Give us this day.* New York, NY: W. W. Norton & Company.

Sullivan, H. S. (1954/1970 edn). *The psychiatric interview.* New York, NY: W. W. Norton & Company.

Sullivan, H. S. (2013). *The interpersonal theory of psychiatry.* Abingdon: Routledge.

Szarkowski, J. (1973). *Looking at photographs: 100 pictures from the collection of the Museum of Modern Art.* New York, NY: The Museum of Modern Art.

Toadvine, T. (2018). Maurice Merleau-Ponty. In *The Stanford encyclopedia of philosophy.* Retrieved from https://plato.stanford.edu/archives/spr2018/entries/merleau-ponty/

Tufte, E. (2006). *Beautiful evidence.* Cheshire, CT: Graphics Press.

Turkle, S. (2007). *Evocative objects: Things we think with.* Cambridge MA: The MIT Press.

Vaughans, K., & Spielberg, W. (Eds). (2014). *The psychology of black boys and adolescents.* New York, NY: Praeger.

Welter, V. M. (2012). *Ernst L. Freud, architect: The case of the modern bourgeois home.* New York, NY: Berghahn Books.

Werner, A. (2002). Edmund Engelman: Photographer of Sigmund Freud's home and offices. *International Journal of Psychoanalysis, 83*(2), 445–451.

Weston, E. (1924/1973). *The daybooks of Edward Weston, Vol. I: Mexico.* New York, NY: Aperture.

Wheelis, A. (1966). *The illusionless man.* New York, NY: Harper Colophon.

Wheelis, A. (1987). *The doctor of desire.* New York, NY: W. W. Norton & Company.

Wheelis, J. (2019). *The known, the secret, the forgotten: A memoir.* New York, NY: W. W. Norton & Company.

Williams, M. (2000). The shrinking lonesome sestina. In M. Strand & E. Boland (Eds), *The making of a poem.* New York, NY: W. W. Norton & Company.

Winnicott, D. W. (1953). Transitional objects and transitional phenomena: A study of the first not-me possession. *The International Journal of Psychoanalysis, 34,* 89–97.

Wolf Man, T. (1958). How I came into analysis with Freud. *Journal of the American Psychoanalytic Association, 6,* 348–352.

Wolfe, T. (1940). *You can't go home again.* New York, NY: Scribner.

Wolfenstein, M. (1966). How is mourning possible? *The Psychoanalytic Study of the Child, 21,* 93–123.

Yalom, I. (2008). *Staring at the sun: Overcoming the terror of death.* San Francisco, CA: Jossey- Bass.

Index

Note: Page numbers in *italics* indicate figures.